An Introduction to the Study of Isaiah

Other titles in the T&T Clark Approaches to Biblical Studies series include:

Introduction to Biblical Studies (Second Edition), Steve Moyise
An Introduction to Revelation, Gilbert Desrosiers
An Introduction to the Johannine Gospels and Letters, Jan van der Watt
An Introduction to the Psalms, Alastair G. Hunter
An Introduction to the Study of Luke Acts, V. George Shillington
An Introduction to the Study of Paul, David G. Horrell
Jesus and the Gospels, Clive Marsh and Steve Moyise
Joshua to Kings, Mary E. Mills
The Old Testament in the New, Steve Moyise
The Pentateuch: A Story of Beginnings, Paula Gooder

An Introduction to the Study of Isaiah

by

JACOB STROMBERG

t&t clark

Published by T&T Clark International
A Continuum Imprint
The Tower Building, 11 York Road, London SE1 7NX
80 Maiden Lane, Suite 704, New York, NY 10038

www.continuumbooks.com

British Library Cataloguing-in-Publication Data
A catalogue record for this book is available from the British Library

ISBN: HB: 978-0-567-54394-3
PB: 978-0-567-36330-5

Library of Congress Cataloging-in-Publication Data
A catalog record for this book is available from the Library of Congress

Typeset by Pindar NZ, Auckland, New Zealand

Contents

For Moshe

Acknowledgments

I gratefully acknowledge Koninklijke Brill NV for permission to use a portion of an article first appearing in their journal: "The Role of Redaction Criticism in the Evaluation of a Textual Variant: Another Look at 1QIsa[a] XXXII 14 (38:21–22)," *DSD* 16 (2009), 155–189.

Abbreviations

OTS	*Oudtestamentische Studiën*
SBLStBL	Society of Biblical Literature Studies in Biblical Literature
SJOT	*Scandinavian Journal of the Old Testament*
SJT	*Scottish Journal of Theology*
VT	*Vetus Testamentum*
VTSup	Supplements to *Vetus Testamentum*
WMANT	Wissenschaftliche Monographien zum Alten und Neuen Testament
ZAW	*Zeitschrift für die alttestamentliche Wissenschaft*

Introduction

For more than two millennia the book of Isaiah has been the object of intense scholarly interest. The prophecies contained therein have preoccupied readers from before the Dead Sea Scrolls on up to the present. There can be little doubt that this prophetic book has had a major impact on the religious mind of both Judaism and Christianity, and therefore the Western tradition more broadly. As a result, a mountain of secondary literature now exists, viewing Isaiah through every methodological lens imaginable. For every new method employed in biblical studies, there arises at least one new monograph on Isaiah, subjecting it to yet another perspective. While sorting through this vast sea of analysis will prove itself a challenge for most, it will be especially difficult for those toward the beginning of their studies in biblical literature, the primary audience of the present book. In writing this introduction to Isaiah, I have endeavored to get at the heart of the major issues now facing scholars who study the book. While making every effort to make the discussion accessible, I have also sought to keep it substantive. If I have succeeded, this work should also profit those who have advanced beyond this beginning stage in their studies.

Seeking to address the central issues in Isaianic study in a substantive way requires selectivity. At points breadth has had to give way do depth. It is impossible to discuss meaningfully every possible approach to Isaiah in a work of this length. A comprehensive treatment is simply out of the question. What this book does offer is an examination of the issues that scholars have returned to time and again in recent years, and it does so in a manner that relates the differing perspectives employed. A basic assumption of the present work is, therefore, that many approaches to Isaiah can be related to one another in a logical way. For example, how one examines the theology of Isaiah depends on how one examines the literature of Isaiah, and that depends on what sorts of questions one is putting to that literature. Thus, I have written the book so that its chapters unfold in a meaningful sequence with an underlying argument. While each chapter can be consulted by itself, the reader will profit most from the book by following its train of thought from beginning to end.

Before summarizing the shape of our study, we must first introduce an assumption central to everything that follows: Isaiah the prophet did not write Isaiah the book. While some scholars continue to resist this perspective for theological reasons, it is now widely accepted, permeating most treatments of the book. This point has rightly won wide support. However, it is now necessary to begin explaining the reasons for this view with a positive claim — that some of the prophecies in the book are actually authentic. With traditional historical-critical scholarship, I employ the terms "authentic" and "secondary," the former referring to the oracles deemed to stem from the prophet himself and the latter to those thought to derive from a later hand. But unlike much of traditional historical-critical scholarship, I do not attach a value judgment to these terms. Here "authentic" is not better than "secondary." This of course follows a broader shift in biblical studies where later developments are now being appreciated as much as original sources. The rendering is now as important as that which is rendered, so that scholars are now just as interested in the *presentation* of the prophet Isaiah as they are in the actual *person* of the prophet. At any rate, while some might wish to deny anything in the book to Isaiah of Jerusalem, this position seems improbable (Williamson 2004). As has traditionally been held by those who view the book as the product of later hands, there are good reasons to see parts of chs. 1–39 as having stemmed from the prophet himself, many of the oracles in these chapters being firmly rooted in the eighth-century Assyrian context of Isaiah's day (Dever 2007, Machinist 1983). Therefore, the origins of the book of Isaiah ultimately lead back to the prophet Isaiah.

That said, beginning in the eighteenth century, many scholars no longer felt that Isaianic authorship of the whole book was the best explanation for what they found therein. This judgment arose for a variety of reasons and applied especially to the latter half of the book, chs. 40–66. It is everywhere evident in these chapters that they *presuppose* rather than *predict* the Babylonian destruction of Jerusalem and Judean exile, a series of events which occurred long after Isaiah's death. A case in point is the long poem towards the end of the book at 63.7–64.12. Rather than being any sort of prophecy, this poem has the form of a lament wherein a voice recounts the kind of divine deeds of the past as a basis for asking God to act in the present state of oppression. That present from which the speaker laments is clearly after the destruction of Jerusalem at the hands of the Babylonians.

> Our holy and beautiful house,
> > where our ancestors praised you,
> has been burnt with fire,
> > and all our pleasant places have become ruins.
> After all this, will you restrain yourself, O Lord?
> > Will you keep silent and punish us so severely? (64.11-12)

There is no prediction here; only lamentation leading to supplication, supplication for restoration after Babylonian invasion when the temple was destroyed. Thus, Isa. 63.7–64.12 no more presents itself as authored by the prophet Isaiah than Deuteronomy 34 claims for itself Mosaic authorship ("no one knows his [Moses'] burial place to this day" [v. 6]).

Several other passages in the latter half of the book show that it *presumes* rather than *predicts* such a setting. Here are a few examples. In 48.20, the people are told: "come out of Babylon, flee from the Chaldeans." This is an imperative, not a prediction, and the imperative only makes sense if spoken to a people already in exile in Babylon. In 40.1-2, the imperative goes forth to "comfort my people . . . speak tenderly to Jerusalem." The basis of this command is that Jerusalem "has received double for all of her sins," clearly a reference to the exile spoken of throughout 40–55 where the people are offered comfort. Comfort can now be proclaimed because the people have paid for their sin through destruction and exile. Again, the exile is presupposed rather than predicted. The imperative ("comfort") is spoken out of this context. Finally, there are passages wherein God says he is responsible for raising up Cyrus (e.g. 45.1), the Persian king who conquered Babylon and allowed the exiles to return home. For these reasons and others, scholars have rightly concluded that 40–66 stem from a much later author than Isaiah of Jerusalem. The argument here is not that prediction of different sorts is impossible and that therefore all of these references in 40–66 must have been written after the fact. That would be a misunderstanding of what has been said. Rather, the argument is that 40–66 *presumes* rather than *predicts* the Babylonian exile, setting its authorship in a time far later than Isaiah the prophet.

This conclusion regarding authorship has been further refined, the most significant development being that 56–66 are now widely regarded as stemming from a hand later than that responsible for 40–55. Very briefly, there are at least three reasons scholars posit this further separation. First, both sections presuppose a different historical situation. Isaiah 40–55 seems to have been written on the cusp of the end of the exile. Hence, there are the references to Cyrus alongside the imperative to come out of Babylon, both of which were just noted. By contrast, Isaiah 56–66 assumes a later situation where the people seem to have returned to the land and the rebuilding of the temple was underway or complete (e.g. 56.1-8; 66.1-2, 20). Thus, 56–66 appear to have been written after 40–55. Second and in line with this, 56–66 depend literarily on 40–55, which they develop through allusion. As we shall see later, 56–66 shows every sign of having been written by someone who read and *interpreted* 40–55, so that it appears the two sections had separate authors. Third, while hardly determinative on its own, there is also the fact that both sections differ stylistically in some respects, reinforcing the impression created by the first two points.

As a result, it is now common to refer to Isaiah in terms of a three-part structure in discussions of its authorship. (1) "First-Isaiah" and "Proto-Isaiah" (PI) are terms used interchangeably to refer to chs. 1–39 which are thought to preserve material that stems from the eighth-century Judean prophet, Isaiah. (2) "Second-Isaiah" and "Deutero-Isaiah" (DI) are terms used interchangeably to designate chs. 40–55 which are thought to stem from a figure active toward the end of the Babylonian exile. (3) "Third-Isaiah" and "Trito-Isaiah" (TI) are terms used interchangeably to refer to chs. 56–66 which are thought to stem from the post-exilic period, after the return from Babylon. We shall see later that the formation of the book is much more complex than this three-fold designation might imply. Nevertheless, these are the terms that have developed in discussions of Isaiah's authorship, and they do reflect certain realities about the work itself.

To many the idea that the prophet did not write the book bearing his name may come as a surprise. After all, the book does begin in 1.1: "The vision of Isaiah son of Amoz which he saw concerning Judah and Jerusalem in the days of Uzziah, Jotham, Ahaz, and Hezekiah, kings of Judah." While this is not the place for a full discussion of all of the differences between our ideas of authorship as moderns and those of the ancient Israelites, it may help to say just a few words about this here. Clearly, the ancient Israelites, at least those responsible for biblical literature, did not regard it as inappropriate to supplement a pre-existing work while remaining anonymous. Take, for example, the passage mentioned above, Deuteronomy 34. Most scholars regard this as a later addition to Deuteronomy, perhaps with an eye toward the Pentateuch as a whole (Chapman 2000: 113–131). Most likely the author of this passage will have regarded the legal corpus he inherited and to which he made his addition as stemming from that great figure of the past, Moses. Nevertheless, in supplementing that older corpus with Deuteronomy 34, this later hand felt no need to identify himself as author, and this despite the fact that his addition made no claim of Mosaic authorship for itself either (v. 6). As a result, he allowed his contribution in Deuteronomy 34 to remain anonymous, bearing neither his name nor that of Moses.

Thus, there exists a real cultural difference as regards authorship between ancient Israel and many modern societies. The nature of authorship was simply different. It is in this light that our discussion of Isaianic authorship should be seen. But what sort of claim were the later editors and authors of the Isaianic tradition making for their work vis-à-vis the original oracles? How will they have seen their role in the formation of the book? One explanation very much born out by the evidence is that of Seitz, who says regarding the title in 1.1 that it "functions as a super-scription for the entire book. What 1:1 states, however, is less a matter of authorship or proprietary claims made on behalf of Isaiah than it is a statement of belief, made on the part of those who shaped the Isaiah traditions, that what followed was a faithful rendering of the essence of Isaiah's preaching as vouchsafed to him by God" (1993: 24).

It will be noticed from the above that the three parts of Isaiah reflect three key periods in Israel's history, the pre-exilic, exilic, and post-exilic periods. It might be helpful briefly to summarize the relevant events in these periods, though the student can find this information readily in most commentaries, study Bibles, or dictionary articles on the book. The major events assumed by the book are as follows (adapted from Sweeney

2010: 965–967). Three episodes in eighth-century Judean history, the time and place of the prophet's activity, show up in chs. 1–39. Each of these historical episodes relates to the increased imperial interests of Assyria over the Levant (the eastern coast of the Mediterranean) where Judah and Israel were situated. Beginning in 735 B.C.E. Pekah, the king of Israel, and Rezin, the king of Syria (Damascus or Aram), sought the support of Ahaz, the king of Judah, in an effort to repel the Assyrian encroachment into their territory. They were unsuccessful at gaining Judah's support. As a result the coalition formed by Israel and Syria (the Syro-Ephraimite coalition) came against Judah, seeking to install a more compliant king in Jerusalem. Ahaz appealed to Assyria for help and was delivered. However, Judah then became a vassal of Assyria, which shortly proved problematic for the country. Following this, the Assyrians began taking control of the Levant, capturing Syria and in 722 overthrowing the northern kingdom of Israel. Later, during a change in Assyrian leadership, Hezekiah, king of Judah, rebelled, and in 701 the Assyrians came down on Judah, destroying some of the cities around Jerusalem which was itself spared at the cost of a payment of tribute.

The latter half of the book of Isaiah reflects two events later in Israel's history, both related to the next two imperial powers who asserted their interests in the Levant after Assyria. Eventually, the Babylonian empire replaced the Assyrians, and Judah came under their control. When Zedekiah, the last king of Judah, rebelled against the Babylonians, the outcome was the destruction of Jerusalem and its temple, as well as the deportation of much of the population (in 586). Thus began the period of the Babylonian exile which is presupposed in chs. 40–55. Nearly 50 years later, Cyrus conquered Babylon, ensuring Persia's position as the new world empire (in 539). Shortly after his victory, Cyrus issued a decree that the Jews be allowed to return home and begin rebuilding their temple. Some of the exiles did return and rebuild. Somewhere in this period chs. 56–66 were written.

Before turning to the body of our analysis, we should first briefly summarize its shape and contents. The first three chapters deal with the formation of the book of Isaiah. If the book we now have is composite, being written by more than one author, then we are confronted with the issue of its formation: what was the process which led from the original oracles of Isaiah of Jerusalem to the 66-chapter book now before us? Chapter 1 outlines different scholarly interests in asking this question, as well as the methods used to get at an answer. It then examines what scholars have said about the formation of chs. 1–39, moving from the exilic and post-exilic stages of this material back to its pre-exilic shape and some of the issues involved in reconstructing that early layer. This chapter having raised the question as to who was responsible for the exilic and post-exilic editing of 1–39, Chapters 2 and 3 take this up with an examination of DI (40–55) and TI (56–66) respectively. In each case the formation of the section itself is considered before its relationship to PI is examined (1–39). For example, I consider the formation of DI before discussing what scholars have said about its relation to PI. Highlighting different approaches, I suggest, in line with recent scholarship, that the authors of DI and TI each had a role in editing an earlier form of PI. From these discussions of Isaiah's editing the conclusion emerges that the message of Isaiah the prophet, whose name the book now bears, has been made to be seen through the lens of exile and restoration; these pivotal moments in Israel's history, now textualized, have become a key part of the structure of the book.

Chapters 4 and 5 shift the discussion away from formation and toward questions of reading. If the book had such a formation, then what does that suggest for how it was to be read? Chapter 4 directs its attention to those studies seeking a "literary approach" to Isaiah. Here, I conclude that a literary approach is at root a discourse-oriented approach, in that it seeks to make sense of the patterns of meaning found in the text, rather than inquire into the realities behind it, an interest belonging to source-oriented analysis. After surveying several features in Isaiah that are clearly literary, I conclude with others that Isaiah is a piece of literature. Thus, as a literary text, Isaiah merits a literary approach. Since it is seen that literary approaches to Isaiah invariably have at their heart an interest in reading the book holistically, Chapter 5 goes on to discuss the different bases scholars propose for doing this. In particular, I treat various proposals for reading Isaiah as a meaningful whole even though it is composite. I ask: if Isaiah reflects many intentions, being written by many hands, then isn't it just an anthology, rather than a single book? Here it becomes important to recognize the carefully considered literary strategies woven into this composite work, strategies arising from theological assumptions deeply ingrained in the world view of the book's final editors.

The last two chapters round off the book with a consideration of Isaiah's theology. Chapter 6 examines what various studies mean by "the theology of Isaiah" by identifying the different methodological avenues chosen. Do scholars mean "theology" in a descriptive or a confessional sense? Are they merely describing what is there, or are they committed to it as religious persons? Do they approach "Isaiah" in a source- or a discourse-oriented manner? Are they aiming at an earlier form of the book, or the book as we have it? I explore these two sets of alternatives through examples of their various combinations: descriptive/source-oriented, descriptive/discourse-oriented, confessional/source-oriented, and confessional/discourse-oriented. Lastly, Chapter 7 seeks to offer a discourse-oriented analysis of two Isaianic themes that were of special theological significance both to the editors of the book and to its later readers — the destiny of Zion in the prophet's message and, in the light of this, the scope of the royal promises.

Chapter 1

The Formation of First-Isaiah

1. Introduction

In the introduction to this book, I noted widespread agreement that the book of Isaiah was not written by the prophet Isaiah — that it is composite, being the product of differing hands at work over a long period of time. As was noted, scholars believe that chs. 1–39 preserve material from Isaiah himself, that chs. 40–55 stem from the late exilic age, and that chs. 56–66 were composed even later in the period after the return. If this is correct, then the book of Isaiah is not unlike a patch-work quilt, in that, pieces from differing origins have been sewn together into a single work. Such a composite work naturally raises the question: how did the book come together into what we now have? What was the process which led from the original oracles of Isaiah of Jerusalem to the 66-chapter book now before us? Over the past 30 years, this question has attracted renewed attention (see the surveys in Höffken 2004 and Williamson 2009).

While some may find the formation of the book of Isaiah interesting in and of itself, I suspect most have sought to understand it in an effort to illuminate two further issues whose clarification depends on this. One of these concerns the historical prophet — namely, what did the prophet Isaiah preach? To get at this, scholars separate material thought to be "original" — that is, that comes from the prophet himself — from material thought to have originated from some other later source, being in this sense "secondary." Obviously, this whole procedure requires a clear understanding of the formation of the book, since it is that understanding which guides in no small measure the decision to assign material to "original" and "secondary" layers. Once one has distinguished and dated all of the various layers found in the book, it should be possible (at least in theory) to reconstruct the preaching of the historical Isaiah, or of the exilic prophet behind 40–55, or of any other hand whose work is now found in the book (provided they had a "preaching" ministry to begin with). While the results of such research often differ and certainly do not always persuade, this goal remains a legitimate reason to understand the formation of the book.

The other reason scholars would like to grasp the book's formation has less to do with reconstructing the preaching (or beliefs) of an individual in a particular period of ancient Israelite history and more to do with how this preaching was to be read once it was written down, commented upon, and collected together with other oracles into a book. How was this new literary context to serve as a guide for the reader of the older oracles? To take the broadest possible example, many scholars are now asking: how was one meant to read the oracles of Isaiah of Jerusalem in the context of the book as a whole which contains material from the later exilic and post-exilic periods? How, if at all, was this larger literary context to have guided the readers for whom the older oracles had been preserved? Many scholars interested in this question believe that a clearer understanding of the formation of the book will shed light on how those who made it intended it to be read, a point that will be addressed in Chapters 4 and 5.

Despite the picture sometimes drawn, these two interests need not be seen in conflict. The peeling away of layers to get at the original words of a prophet differs from (rather than competes with) asking how those words were to be read in the context of a book incorporating much later material. In fact, asking the one question can illuminate the other. However one views the relationship between these two different tasks, it is widely agreed that both require an understanding of how the book reached its present form, and that is the subject of this and the next two chapters.

Before looking at some of the particular issues and proposals concerning the formation of the book of Isaiah, we should first note that scholarship has undergone significant revision as regards this issue. Up until about 30 years ago, it was common practice to treat Isaiah 1–39 in more or less complete isolation from 40–66. This was based on a theory developed in the latter part of the eighteenth century and given its definitive form in the nineteenth century by Bernhard Duhm (1892). According to Duhm, 40–55, and later 56–66, were written up entirely independently of 1–39, a section which had a long editorial history that, despite seeing the addition of material from the periods when 40–55 and 56–66 came into existence (the exilic and post-exilic periods respectively), had occurred independently of these later sections in the book. The result was that 1–39 and 40–66 consisted of two collections that had developed separately from one another, and were joined together only at a very late stage. Duhm did not argue at length for the process by which they were combined, since he (like most in his day) focused his efforts in the first instance on showing that the book was composite — a point still very much under debate at the time. The upshot of such scholarly efforts was that 1–39 was seen for a long time as having very little to do with 40–66; hence they were often treated in isolation from each other in monographs and commentaries (see the survey in Seitz 1991: 1–35); some exceptions to this trend are listed in Williamson (1994: 1–18).

Most scholars now understand the composite nature of the book differently. For them, while chs. 40–66 still contain exilic and post-exilic material, so that they cannot have been written by the hand responsible for the pre-exilic sections of 1–39, these two parts of the book are no longer viewed as having developed independently from one another. Scholars have argued this in two ways, each of which will receive greater attention below. On the one hand, there is now a strong consensus that 40–66 were written up in light of, and as a conscious development of, some form of 1–39. On the other hand, there is now also a growing body of scholarship which finds evidence that at least certain stages in the editing of 1–39 were undertaken in light of 40–66, and in some instances by the same hand involved in the composition of the latter. This, of course, is not a return to the older view that the eighth-century Isaiah was the author of the whole book; these scholars still find multiple hands at work in the book. This position does, however, find the view inadequate which sees 1–39 and 40–66 as having developed independently from one another. Scholars are finding far too many textual connections between these two parts of the book to continue maintaining their independence. This aspect of the redaction of 1–39 is touched on below, but receives a fuller treatment in the next two chapters.

2. Methodological Considerations

All of this is likely to raise an obvious question: how can one get at the formation of the book if all we have is the end product of this process — the present final form? By what means can scholars perceive depth in a text, and then reconstruct a history of its development? After all, it is not as if we actually possess any of the earlier stages in the formation of the book which scholars have posited. These, if they ever existed in the form supposed, have been lost to history. Before one dismisses the enterprise altogether, however, it should be remembered that theories of the book's formation have been built around specific details in the text, and those details are not going to go away. Scholars make observations on the text, and infer from these how it reached its present form. The whole process may be referred to as "informed speculation."

The sort of observations I have in mind here are those used in "redaction criticism" — that is, the study of how texts were "edited" in ancient Israel. In general terms, such editing could entail the (re-)arrangement of pre-existing sources, as well as the composition of fresh material alongside them (see Barton 1992). Such observations are employed in tracing the formation of Isaiah. Since many of these observations are readily apparent in the following discussions, I list only some of the most important points here: (1) A single book may contain material whose assumed historical background differs from one passage to the next such that a single author could not have composed the whole from scratch. In this case, the historical background assumed by a passage may help to distinguish it from another passage in the same book. One could note, for example, that Isaiah 40–55 assumes the Babylonian exile has taken place, whereas some material in 1–39 assumes an earlier period before the exile, when

Assyria ruled. This observation allows scholars to distinguish the material in terms of authorship, while enabling them to discern which of it was written earlier and which of it later.

(2) Because many biblical books (including Isaiah) were not composed from scratch, but used pre-existing sources, their literary character often includes rough edges. To return to our earlier comparison, Isaiah is like a patch-work quilt, in that it is made of different pieces. Where these different pieces join, one often finds a rough edge, a disjuncture in the text better explained as the result of editing pre-existing material than wholly new composition. Scholars will differ in their judgments as to what constitutes a disjuncture, and whether or not any one particular rough edge points to a composite feature of the text; but such edges exist, and the Hebrew text of Isaiah abounds with them. Take, for example, the odd shift in number at Isa. 1.29: "For *they* will be ashamed of the terebinths *you* desired." In the context, one clearly expects the reading "you will be ashamed," which is in fact what many translations give, but not what the Hebrew text has. Along with other observations, this shift in person may suggest that a pre-existing source (vv. 29-31 in the second person) has been attached via a comment (vv. 27-28 in the third person) to the preceding oracle concerning Jerusalem's fate in vv. 21-27. Such disjunctures often align with observations on differing historical contexts. In this example, it is frequently noted that vv. 27-31 reflect historical realities spoken of in the post-exilic TI, but reflected nowhere else in PI (Williamson 2006: 145–162).

(3) In conjunction with these first two points, one often finds, in addition, differences in style, language, or theological outlook. In Isaiah 60–62, for example, scholars note the lack of any divine speech formulae (e.g. "thus says the Lord") which, however, abound in 56–59 and 65–66. While occasionally it is possible to explain such differences in terms of the strategy of a single author, this is not always the case; sometimes they do not appear to serve any particular function. When this is so, attention to editorial features of the text can often explain the shift. Thus, in the case of 60–62 just noted, scholars observe in conjunction with the distribution of these divine speech formulae that the outlook of this material differs considerably from that around it, concluding that these (and still other features noted) are best explained on the hypothesis that 60–62 formed an earlier core of material around which much of the rest of TI was later added (see, for example, Smith 1995).

(4) One feature of book formation in ancient Israel that has received renewed attention in recent years is known in German scholarship as *Fortschreibung*. This refers to a phenomenon wherein a scribe or editor writes up new material in light of, and onto, the pre-existing sources he is working with (Steck 1991b). Thus, the new composition will allude to the old in some way. It will be seen below, for example, that TI alludes to material from throughout 1–55. By studying such allusions (or textual dependencies) scholars are able to gain further leverage on which texts came first and which came later in the whole process of formation.

(5) The last principle to be mentioned is probably the most important,

and this is the cumulative nature of arguments about the formation of a passage or book. While it is probably always possible to find an alternative explanation for any one of the features listed above when that feature stands alone — making an appeal to editing unnecessary —, such an explanation becomes increasingly improbable the more such features appear in a single passage. When several of these features appear, a cumulative case begins to emerge wherein each adds weight to the other — so that an editorial explanation arises as the most plausible one.

These are some of the observations, at any rate, which scholars seek to employ in explaining the formation of a book like Isaiah. All of this may seem complicated, but Isaiah is a complicated book — no doubt part of its attraction to readers over the past two millennia.

Some would object to this whole line of questioning, arguing that it is highly speculative and that we ought therefore to read the book without any reference to its history of development. That sort of reading I do not wish to challenge; after all, it is hard to imagine that the ancient authors of the book required their readers to reconstruct its full history of development before they were able to get the point. Moreover, that such inquiry is speculative cannot be gainsaid. However, to use this as an objection to the whole body of research that has grown up around the question of Isaiah's formation does not seem balanced in my opinion. There are certain points which are widely agreed, and seem to have a solid basis in the evidence. Moreover, since one's preconceptions about how the book came to be will affect one's reading of it (at least for many people), a more sensible approach would seem to be to make of the available evidence what one can, to recognize that the result will be more akin to "informed speculation" than "absolute fact," and then to see how such an approach can and cannot illuminate exegesis of the text (if that is one's goal to begin with). The fact is that nearly all scholars agree that Isaiah is a composite work (and for good reason), and this will inevitably raise the question as to how the book came to form the present whole we now have in chs. 1–66.

The remainder of this chapter will address some of the main problems and proposals for the formation of Isaiah 1–39. It will be recalled that Duhm separated the book into three parts: PI, DI, and TI. Theories of the book's formation have tended to work themselves out within the framework of this threefold division. Because of this scheme's great influence on later scholarship, and because it does accurately capture certain features of the literature itself, our survey will take it as a rough-and-ready guide in what follows in this and the next two chapters. It goes without saying that space requires that this survey be selective. I hope, however, to capture the main issues at play.

3. The Formation of First-Isaiah

As the introduction to our study indicated, there are good reasons to suppose that Isaiah 1–39 preserves an early collection of prophecies from Isaiah of Jerusalem. It is difficult to know precisely what this early collection of "authentic" Isaianic material may have looked like before it was edited into the book we now have. But there is a measure of agreement on what may have been some of the major steps in this editorial process: scholars have found secondary material in 1–39 from the post-exilic, exilic, and pre-exilic periods. Our description will work from the end of this process back toward its beginning, that is, from the post-exilic back to the pre-exilic shape of this material as it has been conceived of by scholarship. In what follows, I will not always make a distinction between exilic and post-exilic material, and will often opt instead to describe something simply as stemming from the exile or after. The reason is that, while it is frequently possible to distinguish clearly between pre-exilic and exilic/post-exilic material in Isaiah, a much finer judgment is often required to differentiate between exilic and post-exilic material. This can be a finer judgment for any number or reasons, one being that even texts written after the exile — after Cyrus' proclamation in 538 B.C.E. that the Jews be allowed to return home — may look forward to yet a further return. The authors of such passages still regarded "exile" as a reality not yet fully resolved with the events immediately following Cyrus' proclamation (e.g. 56.8; 66.20). While the following survey will give some consideration to the idea that these exilic/post-exilic stages in the formation of 1–39 stemmed from hands also at work in 40–66, that question will be treated mainly in the next two chapters.

a. Exilic and Post-exilic Stages in the Formation of First-Isaiah

While scholars can disagree quite sharply over what exactly should be regarded as exilic or post-exilic within chs. 1–39, most of them would agree that such material exists in each of its major sections. The two sections, concerning which there is perhaps most agreement on this point, are the so-called apocalyptic collections: 24–27 (the "Isaiah Apocalypse") and 34–35 (the "Little Apocalypse" ["Little" because it is smaller than the other one]).

As the name of each suggests, these sections have been viewed through the lens of the development of apocalyptic literature (e.g. Daniel, Enoch, Revelation). Since such literature with its particular mode of thought first appeared quite late in Israel's history (third–second centuries B.C.E.), the association has generally implied a late date for these two Isaianic texts. Chapters 24–27 have lent themselves to this association because they contain "a view of the future which has a universal, not just national or even international, scope (e.g. 24.21, 25.7-8); and they envisage manifestations of God's power in the cosmic as well as the political sphere" (Barton 1995: 90). Chapters 34–35 also display elements of apocalyptic, though far fewer than 24–27. Isaiah 34.1-4, for example, describes the judgment to fall on all the nations (v. 2) wherein the "host of heaven shall rot away, and all the heavens shall roll up like a scroll" (v. 4). The punishment of the host of heaven here, and their imprisonment in 24.21-22, may be compared with the same in 1 Enoch 18, a chapter from a late apocalyptic writing. Characterizing these Isaianic passages as apocalyptic has not gone unchallenged, however. Much of the debate depends on how one defines "apocalyptic" to begin with (see Collins 1992: 284).

Regardless of how one resolves the relationship of Isaiah 24–27 and 34–35 to the development of apocalyptic, scholars regard these collections as exilic, or post-exilic, for quite another reason. Both presuppose material in the book that itself has an exilic, or post-exilic, date. In order for the collections in 24–27 and 34–35 to presuppose such material, they must either be contemporaneous with it — that is, be written by the same author — or be later than it, depending on it literarily. In either case, they stem from a stage in the formation of PI during the exile or later.

Scholars have long recognized that Isaiah 24–27 borrows from other scriptural texts (including Isaiah), a recognition that has increased in recent years (see Polaski 2001, and Hibbard 2006). One such borrowing from Isaiah comes in 27.2-6 which describes how one will "sing" to a "vineyard" that the Lord is to keep "day and night." On that day Jacob would take root, blossom, and fill the world with fruit (v. 6). It is widely agreed that the author of this passage has borrowed from "the song of the vineyard" in 5.1-7. Here the prophet vows to "sing" of a "vineyard" which the Lord had tended, but which had not yielded the grapes he desired, bringing upon itself divine judgment. (Verse 7 identifies the vineyard as Israel and Judah.) The point of the allusion seems to be that the wrath incurred by the vineyard in 5.1-7 was now at its end in 27.2-6 ("I have no wrath" [v. 4]). In the former passage, God vows to withhold rain from his vineyard and cease tending it so that "thorns and briars" appear, whereas in the latter, he promises to water it "every moment" and march out in war should there be "thorns and briars." Whatever the precise meaning of this allusion, it illustrates how chs. 24–27 borrow from other earlier Isaianic passages. But since "the song of the vineyard" in 5.1-7 is generally thought to stem from Isaiah himself, this allusion need not imply the exilic (or later) date that many have assigned to 24–27. In theory, ch. 27 could depend on ch. 5, but still originate from a pre-exilic setting.

However, such an explanation is not possible for all of the allusions in 24–27, since some of these depend literarily on passages in 40–66, thereby indicating just such a late date for the "Isaiah Apocalypse." One allusion thought to fall into this category comes in 26.17-18 where the people liken themselves to a woman in the midst of childbirth: "as a pregnant woman draws near to giving birth, she writhes and cries out in her pains, so we were before you, O Lord; we were pregnant, we writhed, we gave birth to wind; we have wrought no victories on the earth." This looks as if it could be taking up 66.7-9 which employs similar birthing language to encourage the hearers that their salvation is near: "For Zion writhes, she gives birth to her children. Will I bring to the breach, but not deliver, says the Lord." According to Hibbard, "The birth imagery of 66:7-9 is redeployed in 26:17-18 to show that Jerusalem's imminent restoration and prosperity have not materialized . . ." (2006: 159). If this direction of dependence is correct, then 26.17-18 must be at least post-exilic, the period which saw the composition of chs. 56–66.

However, chs. 24–27 are not usually seen as having been composed from the very beginning. Rather, this collection is generally regarded as composite. This obviously introduces a further element of uncertainty into dating this material, but that should not be allowed to cloud the overall picture that has emerged from studies of these chapters: such allusions to other scriptural texts (including Isaiah) are to be found *throughout* the whole of 24–27. These allusions give this collection a semblance of unity, but also, because many of them refer to texts that are exilic or later, a sense that the whole should be dated quite late. It is hardly surprising, therefore, that the whole collection is rounded off with a promise of return from exile in 27.12-13. Many have suggested that an editor placed 24–27 after the oracles against the nations in 13–23, in order to draw those oracles into a universal and cosmic frame of reference.

Chapters 34–35 are also thought to presuppose material from elsewhere in the book that dates to exilic times or later. Most scholars have treated chs. 34 and 35 as two sides of the same coin, the former announcing judgment on all nations especially Edom (perhaps a cipher for any enemy of God) and the latter promising salvation for Zion — a contrast developed through several parallels (e.g. 34.9//35.6; 34.13//35.7; 34.15-16//35.8-10). The dependence of these chapters on late material is especially clear in 35, which is widely recognized as borrowing from DI (see Mathews 1995 and Hagelia 2006). We could note, for example, some close parallels with ch. 40: the references to the "desert" and "steppe" (35.1//40.3); the promise that many will "see" the "glory of the Lord" (35.2//40.5); and the command "do not fear" because "behold" the Lord "will come" (35.4//40.9-10). The most striking example of such borrowing comes in 35.10 which cites 51.11:

> And the ransomed of the Lord will return; they will come to Zion with rejoicing, and everlasting gladness will be upon their heads. Joy and gladness will overtake them, and grief and sighing will flee away.

In this instance, not only does ch. 35 cite ch. 51 — an exilic passage — but, in doing so, it also looks forward to a "return" from exile — both moves suggesting a late date for the passage. Of course, such parallels between ch. 35 and DI have long been recognized, and at one time it was not uncommon to explain them in terms of common authorship. Many scholars thought DI wrote ch. 35, an explanation still held by some. However, a majority now sees these parallels in terms of the sort of borrowing described here, not least because ch. 35 seems to develop these citations beyond DI, by combining them, for example, with phrases drawn from TI. In this connection, scholars often compare 35.8-10 with 62.10-12, a passage which also anticipates a "redeemed" and "holy" people returning on a "highway." We could also note that in both 35.2 and 60.13 "the glory of Lebanon" will be given for restoration (a phrase not found in DI). Subtle differences such as this appear often enough in ch. 35 to suggest that it looks back to DI in literary dependence. In any case, whether it was written by the author of DI, or stems from a later hand (which seems probable), ch. 35 is clearly exilic or later.

While the case for ch. 34 is less clear, scholars have also noted close parallels between it and TI that suggest a similar scenario. For example, the oracle against Edom in 63.1-6 may have influenced 34.5-8 (note the "day of the Lord's vengeance" in v. 8 and its parallels in 63.4; 61.2); the fate of the rebels in 66.24 may have influenced that of Edom in 34.10 — in both, their fire "will not be extinguished"). Some have also found evidence to suggest that ch. 34 may have been patterned on the oracle against Babylon in ch. 13, an oracle often dated to the exilic period (see below). (Compare, for example, 13.20 with 34.17.) Regarding the placement of ch. 35 (and to a lesser extent ch. 34), it is generally thought that this material was composed to aid the reader in connecting the two halves of the book, 1–39 and 40–66. It was to function as a literary "bridge" of sorts.

Besides the "apocalyptic" collections (24–27 and 34–35), scholars have found many other passages within 1–39 that seem to have been added during or after the exile. One passage that usually also falls into this category is the Hezekiah narrative of 36–39, a story recounting the Assyrian siege on Jerusalem, God's deliverance from it, Hezekiah's sickness and recovery, and the visit of the Babylonian delegation which provokes an announcement of the coming Babylonian exile (Gonçalves 1999, Stromberg 2010: 205–222).

Most would agree that Isaiah 36–39 has been taken from the book of Kings where the same narrative occurs (2 Kgs 18.13–20.19). The two accounts are nearly identical, apart from the addition of a psalm in Isaiah 38 and a few minor changes. Since the book of Kings was probably written (in the form it now has) during the exile or later, the borrowing of this narrative into Isaiah from there must have occurred later, making it a late addition in 1–39. Strengthening this conclusion, we may also observe that Isaiah 36–39 ends with an announcement of exile to Babylon (note the omission of 2 Kgs 20.20-21 from Isaiah) — so that it looks as if the narrative was deliberately placed before chs. 40–66 which assume the exile has taken place. In this way, it is argued, the Hezekiah narrative was to serve as a transition into the remainder of the book, preparing the reader for the exilic context of everything that followed. If the placement of the Hezekiah narrative into Isaiah presupposed some form of chs. 40–66, then it cannot have been added before the exile, the period assumed by this half of the book.

While these two arguments (taken together) form a convincing case for the late dating of Isaiah 36–39, this should not be taken to imply that the narrative itself is a wholly late invention, containing no historical memory of the events. The Kings account, from which the Isaianic version was taken, is itself clearly made up of sources which will have been written up at an even earlier period.

Assigning Isaiah 36–39 to such a late date may carry with it a similar judgment for Isa. 7.1-17, since this passage shows many signs of having been composed in relation to these chapters. There are several cross-references between the two passages that will be discussed in the last chapter of our book. Such cross referencing suggests that 7.1-17 may have been written in connection with 36–39. Moreover, 7.1-17 stands out from those chapters preceding and following it: where 7.1-17 refers to Isaiah in the third person, chs. 6 and 8 refer to him in the first person. Though again, just because this may be a late addition does not mean it lacks any value as an historical source. Many would regard 7.1-17 — the narrative about Ahaz — as having been edited, which of course implies an earlier source.

So far, we have noted three passages that, according to most scholars, stem from a period during or after the exile. Each of these — 24–27, 34–35, and 36–39 — tends to be seen as wholly secondary to an early Isaiah collection. Even 36–39, which we have just noted likely contain traditions that lead back to the prophet himself, have often been spoken of as an historical "appendix" (on analogy with Jeremiah 52 which is thought to have been imported in modified form from 2 Kgs 24.18–25.30). By contrast, much of the rest of 1–39 is thought to have grown from a core of pre-exilic material into its present shape which is to be dated to the exilic period or later. A consequence of this more organic process of development is that it can sometimes be harder to distinguish between "authentic" and "secondary" passages, allowing opinions to differ more sharply over what within this remaining material belongs to this late stage in the formation of 1–39.

Such is a fair description of scholarship on the "oracles concerning the nations" in chs. 13–23, a title which tends to overlook the material dealing with Judah. In these chapters scholars find several "authentic" fragments from the prophet Isaiah, but judge the final form of the collection to have been reached only in the exilic or post-exilic period. That these chapters were to form a collection seems clear by their use of the term "oracle" (*maśśā'*) which is found in nine headings throughout, but only once further in the entire book of Isaiah.

By most accounts, the late editing of this collection can be discerned in its opening oracle (13.1–14.23), the "oracle concerning Babylon which Isaiah son of Amoz saw." Indeed, Sweeney excludes only this passage from his judgment that "all the prophecies concerning foreign nations in chs. 13-23 were composed in relation to the 7th-century Josianic edition of the book of Isaiah (chs. 15-16; 17-18; 19-20; 23) or in the late 8th or early 7th century (21:1-10, 11-12, 13-17; 22:1-25)" (1996: 215). The precise dating of several of these oracles has bedeviled scholarship. One reason for this is, as Clements notes, "Such prophecies, once given, appear in some instances to have been reapplied when later circumstances occasioned the need and opportunity for doing so" (1980: 131). Isaiah 16.13-14, for example, seems to "update" the preceding oracle against Moab. Since most (though not all) scholars can agree on the late date of the oracle concerning Babylon in 13.1–14.23, a few comments on it should serve our purpose.

While at least one serious attempt has been made at ascribing this oracle to the period of Isaiah the prophet (Erlandsson 1970), that has generally not been accepted by scholars who note that the passage assumes Babylon is a major world power — an assumption suitable to the period before 539 B.C.E. at which point Babylon fell to the Persians, but not to the eighth century when it was still only a vassal to Assyria against which it eventually rebelled. Moreover, prior to the waning of the Assyrian empire at the end of the seventh century, the Medes were generally in alliance with the Babylonians, a situation differing from 13.17 which names the Medes as the agent of Babylon's downfall. Most, therefore, continue to view 13.1–14.23 as an exilic composition.

However, even on this view, many, if not most, scholars see the oracle concerning Babylon in 13.1–14.23 as the product of editing rather than as a wholly new composition from scratch. Hence, many would regard the taunt against the king of Babylon in ch. 14 as consisting of a poem (vv. 4b-21) — perhaps originally directed against an Assyrian king in Isaiah's day — to which was added vv. 3-4a, 22-23, prose comments meant to identify the subject of the poem (van Keulen 2010). It is striking that, apart from these comments, there is no mention in the poem itself of Babylon or anything else of a historically specific nature.

We could note a similar situation for the oracle in ch. 13, though here there is less agreement among commentators. Apart from the title in v. 1, nothing is said of Babylon until v. 17, and what comes in between provides very little specification and looks rather more like world judgment than something directed at a specific nation (e.g. vv. 9, 11-14). Moreover, most commentators recognize that the prose comment in 14.1-2 is editorial and that it seeks to draw out the positive implications of the previous poem for Israel: Babylon's fall would mean God's compassion on Israel, the exiles would be restored to their land. Thus, many scholars have found a similar situation in ch. 13 as they have in ch. 14.

It seems probable therefore that earlier sources (whose historical referents were left unspecified) have been put together and shaped by an editor who understood them as referring to the downfall of Babylon and its king, a move fully justified by 14.24-27 which follows and states that the divine plan for Assyria's destruction would apply to "all nations." The impression that the oracle against Babylon in 13.1–14.23 is the work of an editor is strengthened by the fact that it now stands as the introduction to the whole collection of oracles concerning the nations in 13–23. Since ch. 21 already contains an oracle about Babylon (making 13.1–14.23 in a sense unnecessary), and in light of the fact that this opening oracle is longer than any that follow, we may suppose that its placement in such a prominent position at the front of this section was the work of an editor who wanted to emphasize Babylon's importance in the divine plan.

As was noted at the outset, the most probable historical context for such activity would have been just before the fall of Babylon to the Persians, during the period of the exile. And one suspects that the placement of 13.1–14.23 at the head of the oracles against the nations owes itself to the great influence that "Babylonian" material had on shaping the book as a whole, for example, through the incorporation of chs. 40–55 into the earlier Isaianic corpus (cf. Isaiah 47). In fact, Williamson (1994: 156–175) builds a strong case that the author of DI was responsible for this oracle; he draws particular attention to the editorial comment in 14.1-2 which links the oracle in ch. 13 to that in ch. 14, employing language whose similarity to chs. 40–55 is hard to deny. Thus, it seems entirely reasonable to conclude (as many have) that the oracles concerning the nations in chs. 13–23, even if consisting largely of pre-exilic material, underwent an important stage of editing in the exilic period.

With that, we have now noted the late editing of 13–23, as well as the late insertion of 24–27, 34–35. It only remains for us to remark on 1–12 and 28–33, sections of 1–39 which are also regarded as having grown from a pre-exilic core into their present respective forms — a process in each instance usually thought to have come to an end only after the exile.

Scholars generally regard Isaiah 1–12 as a unit reaching its conclusion in ch. 12 with a hymn giving thanks for "salvation." Most of what appears in this collection relates to Judah and Jerusalem, distinguishing it from the succeeding oracles about the nations in 13–23. Few would argue that 1–12 was written up from the very beginning, since these chapters show every sign of having arisen through a process of editing. For example, we could note that, while a title appears in 1.1 — introducing the work as a "vision" of Isaiah son of Amoz — another title is given shortly after this in 2.1, which seems redundant and has been taken as a sign that an earlier collection once began there. Or, it could be noted that 5.25, which contains the refrain "despite all this his anger has not turned back, and his hand is outstretched still," appears to have been separated from passages in chs. 9 and 10, where that refrain occurs again (9.12, 17, 21; 10.4).

While scholars find much in 1–12 that reaches back to the pre-exilic period and to Isaiah himself, they have also discovered clear signs that this material underwent editing in the exilic and post-exilic periods. We have already mentioned 7.1-17 which came in for consideration in this respect because of its close connections to the Hezekiah narrative in 36–39, an insert from Kings that seemed to be aware of Isaiah 40–66.

One clear example where "authentic" Isaianic material in 1–12 has been edited from a post-exilic perspective comes in Isaiah 6. For although most would still regard at least part of this chapter as a genuine first-person account by the prophet himself, they also find evidence that it has been edited from this very late perspective. Proposals for the formation of this chapter differ, but they invariably agree on the last line of the last verse. This line is seen as the product of a later editor who wanted to identify the "stump" of v. 13 as a purified remnant surviving divine judgment on the people.

> Even if a tenth part remain in it,
>   it will be burned again,
> like a terebinth or an oak
>   whose stump remains standing
> when it is felled.
>   The holy seed is its stump. (6.13 NRSV)

Many difficulties surround the translation of this verse. However, one thing seems clear: the comment "the holy seed is its stump" is secondary to it. This comment is a gloss on the word "stump" in the original composition (see Emerton 1982).

If it is secondary to the original composition, then *when* was it added? In answering this, the first thing to note is that, according to the logic of God's answer to Isaiah in vv. 11-13, the "holy seed" was to survive the exile, which is clearly spoken of in v. 11 ("and the Lord will *remove* humans, and the forsakenness in the midst of the land will be great"). Hence, the passage itself suggests the remnant "seed" refers to a community alive during, or after, the exile.

In the light of this, it is surely significant that Ezra 9.2 contains the only other occurrence of the expression "holy seed" in the Old Testament. Because Ezra 9 stems from the post-exilic period, we might expect the same for the addition at the end of Isa. 6.13. That conclusion seems to be supported by the fact that Ezra 9 indicates the phrase "holy seed" finds its origin in that late period. As Fishbane (1985: 115–117) has shown, Ezra 9 combines laws from Deut. 7.1-6 and 23.4-9, providing the rational for the decree that the Jews of Ezra's day should divorce their foreign wives. In the process of combining these laws, it is clear that the expression "holy seed" in Ezra 9.2 has been derived from the phrase "holy nation" in Deut. 7.2-6. In short, Ezra 9 suggests the exegetical origin of the expression "holy seed." If this phrase developed in the post-exilic period, then its use in the gloss on Isa. 6.13 must stem from that time or later, a conclusion which fits nicely with the secondary nature of the line.

To further strengthen this conclusion, we may note that a striking parallel exists between this comment in 6.13 and the last two chapters of the book, 65 and 66. Isaiah 6.13 and 65.9 are the only passages in the book employing the term "seed" to describe a remnant, suggesting a close relationship between the two. One (probable) explanation for this parallel is that the comment in 6.13 was made in connection with this penultimate chapter. Indeed, the last two chapters of the book arguably stem from roughly the same milieu as Ezra 9, which would explain why the expression concerning those who "tremble" at God's "word" occurs only in these two passages in the whole Old Testament (Isa. 66.2, 5; Ezra 9.4). In sum, there is good reason to regard the statement "the holy seed is its stump" as a secondary comment on Isa. 6.13 from the post-exilic period. There are other instances of such late editing in 1–12, some of them quite close to the addition in 6.13 (e.g. 4.2-6). Suffice it to say here that these chapters also owe part of their shape to the literary activity of this late period.

We come lastly to Isaiah 28–33, a section that is materially diverse, but held together by the interjection "woe" found throughout (28.1; 29.1, 15; 30.1; 31.1; 33.1). (The "behold" of 32.1 might have had a similar function.) Within this collection, chs. 28–31 are frequently traced back to Isaiah himself, some of this material referring to a time before the fall of the northern kingdom (28.1-4), but most of it relating to Hezekiah's reign and revolt against the Assyrians. While scholars are divided over whether or not ch. 32 should likewise be treated as authentic, they are in very broad agreement that ch. 33 stems from a later period.

The logic behind the present placement of chs. 28–33 has proven more difficult to discern than that of other sections in 1–39. One theory is that an earlier form of this collection originally followed the oracles against the nations in 13–23, its connection to this material then being broken by the later insertion of 24–27. Whether or not this was the case, we may note that it is not inappropriate for chs. 6–8, chapters recounting Isaiah's activity in the Syro-Ephramite crisis, to be followed in a broad sense by 28–31(33), material from later in his ministry. It may not be coincidence either that these chapters should themselves be followed closely by 36–39 where a key moment in that later ministry is recounted.

The historical setting of Isaiah 33 is sufficiently unclear as to allow scholars to come up with radically different proposals. Roberts (1983) defends Isaianic authorship for the passage, while Kaiser places it in the Hellenistic period (1974: 341–342). At the same time, most, though not dating the passage quite so late as Kaiser, would agree that it does not stem from the prophet, preferring instead a setting sometime in the exilic or post-exilic period.

In support of this, it has been argued by more than one scholar that Isaiah 33 was composed, in a manner similar to chs. 34–35, to look both forward to DI and back to certain texts in PI, in this way forming a sort of literary "bridge" between these two parts of the book (Beuken 2000: 245–246). Attention has been drawn, for example, to the following parallels: 33.20//54.2; 33.5-6a//1.21; and 33.6b//11.2. Among the references to PI that scholars find in 33, the most significant for dating this passage may be that in the first verse. When 33.1 condemns an unnamed tyrant as a "destroyer" who will be "destroyed" and a "treacherous one" against whom others will act "treacherously," it looks like a reference to 21.2 ("the treacherous one acts treacherously and the destroyer destroys"), the context of which speaks of the downfall of Babylon. If such a reference is correct, then it may help identify the tyrant in 33.1 as Babylon, an identification that would likewise indicate that this passage has an exilic setting, at least in its final form (cf. also Hab. 1.13). In that case, the oracles in 28–33 have been rounded off in a manner that anticipates in content, if not in form, the second half of the book.

With that we come to the end of our necessarily selective survey of texts within chs. 1–39 that have been edited in the exilic or post-exilic period. We have seen that each major section within these chapters shows signs of such late literary activity. This conclusion gives rise to further questions. Who added this late material? And can we assign such additions to a single layer of editing? If the above survey is correct, then we would have to reckon with at least two editors, one exilic and the other post-exilic. That would mean at least two layers of editing, though scholars usually find more. We might also ask whether or not such editing had anything to do with the addition first of 40–55 and then later of 56–66 to the earlier Isaianic corpus in 1–39? For, as we noted at the beginning of this chapter, scholars no longer view the development of 1–39 independently from 40–66. In the next two chapters, we will see that several have now made the case that such late additions in the first part of the book were made by precisely the authors of the latter part — that the authors of 40–55 and 56–66 each added his own material in 1–39. Suffice it to say here that editors working in the exilic and post-exilic periods (whoever they were) contributed to the present shape of Isaiah 1–39.

b. Pre-exilic Stages in the Formation of First-Isaiah

What can we say about pre-exilic stages in the formation of 1–39? Any answer to this will be directly affected by how we answer a second question: what material within 1–39 can be regarded as reaching back to the prophet himself, or, if not to the prophet, then at least to the pre-exilic period? This question has not received a uniform answer, though there are some broad points of agreement. This lack of uniformity only highlights the tentative nature of any conclusions we might reach about the precise shape of the Isaianic tradition in the pre-exilic period. At the same time, because there is near universal agreement that 1–39 do preserve material that reaches back to the prophet, it remains an entirely reasonable goal to want to reconstruct such a pre-exilic collection: compare the various attempts at this by Wildberger (2002: 513–693), Barthel (1997), and Becker (1997).

I will focus more narrowly on two points in what follows: (1) I will discuss some of the problems inherent in trying to infer the pre-exilic *shape* of the collection of these oracles from their present edited form; and (2) I will briefly discuss the most widespread, though by no means universally held, theory of the pre-exilic editing of this early collection, namely, the theory of a Josianic redaction.

In terms of method, reconstructing the pre-exilic shape of 1–39 might seem relatively straightforward: remove all exilic and post-exilic additions, and what remains should give us the original collection. In that case and on the basis of what was seen in ch. 2, we could expect the original collection to look something like 1–11 and 28–31(32) — minus later additions — with various original sayings from 13–23. Indeed, the resulting collection is not without some shape. According to most scholars, 1–11 preserve material from Isaiah's early ministry while 28–31 consist largely of oracles from his later career, so that a broadly chronological grouping emerges (though, see, for example, 1.5-9; 28.1-4). One problem with this method of reconstruction is that it overlooks possible post-Isaianic additions to the collection which were made in the pre-exilic period. The possibility of such additions will receive some attention below. If such additions were made, then it is not enough simply to remove material from the exile or later in order to arrive at the original collection. A further layer of redaction — this time from the pre-exilic period — would need to be dealt with.

However, there is a separate and more serious problem facing this approach as regards method. Subtracting later additions and regarding what remains as the original shape of the material only reckons with one of two techniques that redactors employed in shaping Isaiah — the composition of fresh material into or alongside pre-existing sources. The other redactional technique, the *rearrangement* of pre-existing material, remains unaccounted for in this approach. Having removed all later additions, one still needs to consider how the oracles may have been ordered prior to their present arrangement.

To illustrate this point, we should look at the first chapter of the book. According to most scholars, this chapter consists largely of oracles that stem from the prophet himself. Most would also agree that a major exception to this comes in vv. 27-31, which are viewed as one or more additions from the exile or later. For reasons given below, this view is highly probable. If we are interested in reconstructing the pre-exilic shape of 1–39, then clearly these verses must be set aside as the product of a later editor. That leaves us with vv. 1-26 which (minus the title in v. 1) are mostly regarded as authentic. Then does that mean the pre-exilic shape of the Isaiah collection began with 1.2-26 and was followed by 2.1ff.? This is the conclusion which would follow from the approach described above which simply subtracts later additions and takes what is left as the original.

However, that conclusion would not find much support among most commentators. For, while they do view vv. 27-31 as having been composed later than the preceding material (most of which is regarded as authentic), they regard vv. 2-26 as composed of fragments lifted from elsewhere in the pre-exilic Isaianic corpus (Fohrer 1962, Williamson 2006: 7–162). A later editor, they argue, assembled this pre-existing material at the head of the book to provide it with an introduction. That is why, among other things, one finds another title in 2.1. This title would be redundant if, when it was composed, it was preceded by the title in 1.1. Isaiah 2.1 says nothing that is not already stated in 1.1. Rather, it makes greater sense to regard 2.1 as the introductory title of an earlier collection, a collection that was then later given a new introduction through the making of ch. 1, perhaps in connection with further expansions elsewhere in the main body of the book.

That ch. 1 consists of authentic fragments is an important point to emphasize for our purpose. Verses 4-9, for example, are usually dated to around 701 B.C.E. when Sennacherib's army invaded Judah (Emerton 1993: 39). On this occasion, the Assyrians captured many towns, drove out much of the population and besieged, but failed to capture, Jerusalem. Hence, vv. 8-9 state: "the daughter of Zion is left over like a hut in a vineyard . . . Had the Lord of Hosts not left us some survivors, we would have become like Sodom; we would have resembled Gomorrah." Verses 10-17, on the other hand, are usually understood as stemming from an earlier period in Isaiah's ministry. In their present form, however, these verses have been made to follow vv. 4-9, the editor linking the two passages through the references to "Sodom" and "Gomorrah" in vv. 9 and 10 (note the different use of these terms in each instance). If ch. 1 is an assemblage of authentic fragments taken from elsewhere in the pre-exilic collection (as many think), then it is insufficient simply to subtract vv. 27-31 and view vv. 2-26 as an earlier introduction to the book. A redactor has *rearranged* pre-existing sources in producing ch. 1.

While not every authentic passage in 1–39 will have been subject to the same degree of editorial rearrangement as ch. 1, this text does caution against overly simplistic reconstructions of a pre-exilic collection. Even if we can agree on the authenticity of certain passages, discerning their original shape is not a simple matter of subtracting all later additions from the present text and leaving what remains in the same sequence as the result. Editors sometimes rearranged their sources in addition to commenting upon them. For this reason, Williamson, who affirms the validity of reconstructing earlier stages of the text, nevertheless sounds a note of caution: "contrary to the impression which has often been given, the further back through the history of the text's evolution we press, the more hypothetical our conclusions become" (2006: 7). From this, we may draw one further conclusion as regards method in retracing the formation of the book: one must first begin with the present shape of the text before seeking to reconstruct its earlier stages, rather than working the other way around.

At the same time, the present form of 1–39 exhibits some patterns which have quite reasonably been understood as reflecting earlier collections from Isaiah's time, giving us some indication of the shape in which the pre-exilic collection(s) circulated. For example, it has been common scholarly practice to discern in the first-person account of 6.1–8.18 an early memoir (German *Denkschrift*) reflecting on the Syro-Ephraimite war. This was thought to have been written by Isaiah himself and secondarily inserted into an early collection of oracles; the memoir was usually thought to have been worked over by later editors as well. For many, such a hypothesis explained why Isaiah's apparent call came in ch. 6 rather than at the beginning of the book, and why some of the material in ch. 5 looked as if it belonged with passages in chs. 9 and 10 (note, for example, the refrain in 5.25 and 9.12, 17, 21; 10.4 ["despite all this his anger has not turned back, and his hand is outstretched still"]). There was even found a reference to Isaiah's having written the memoir in 8.16-18. While this theory has been enormously popular among scholars, it has been challenged in recent years (see, most recently, de Jong 2007: 54–82). Other explanations have been proposed. For example, perhaps ch. 6 recounts Isaiah's commissioning for a specific task, rather than his initial call. Moreover, it is not impossible that 5.25, rather than being displaced by the insertion of 6.1–8.18 (as the theory maintains), was *intentionally* relocated from chs. 9–10 to its present position. Thus, while many still regard at least some of the first-person material in 6.1–8.18 as authentic, they nevertheless reject the theory in its classical formulation.

Any attempt at reconstructing the pre-exilic shape of the Isaianic tradition must reckon with one further point — the possibility that it passed through the hands of editors in the pre-exilic period itself. Indeed, it is not impossible that the prophet himself acted as the first editor of the oracles, writing them down and gathering them together for posterity (cf. 8.1-4, 16-18; 30.8). Perhaps the most widespread view of the pre-exilic redaction of Isaiah is that proposed by Barth (1977), who posited a seventh-century "Assyria redaction" of the oracles stemming from the prophet Isaiah.

This view, often called the "Josianic redaction" by its supporters, seeks to explain the origin of those passages which speak of the overthrow of Assyria (e.g. 10.24-27; 30.27-33). As the name of the redaction suggests, it originated during the reign of king Josiah shortly before the capitulation of Nineveh (612 B.C.E.), the Assyrian capital city. This would have been long after the prophet Isaiah. According to Sweeney (2001: 236), while scholars disagree to some extent over which texts belong to this redaction, they do agree that

> some form of the book was produced in the late seventh century to justify and to articulate King Josiah's reform measures as the goal of Isaiah ben Amoz's prophet message. To this end, Isaiah's calls for the downfall of the Assyrian empire (e.g., Isa 10:5-34) and the rise of the house of David (e.g., Isa 9:1-6; 11:1-9) were to be realized in the reign of Josiah, who freed Judah from its status as an Assyrian vassal and attempted to reestablish an independent Davidic monarchy.

As Sweeney also recognizes, this theory has not proven itself equally convincing to all. To point out one possible objection to it, we could note that nowhere does this material explicitly mention Josiah — an observation which is not insurmountable, but is surely striking, given that the whole point of the redaction was to support his reforms. The lack of any mention of his name here may be contrasted with 1 Kgs 13.1-2 which presents itself as a prediction of Josiah's reform, citing his name 300 years before the event (recounted in 2 Kgs 23.15-18). In the light of this, we might have expected pro-Josianic redactors of the Isaiah tradition to have named him. At the same time, it must be said that the theory has enjoyed a fair degree of support, so that it ought to be taken seriously in any attempt at reconstructing the pre-exilic shape of the Isaiah tradition. A recent overview can be found in de Jong (2007: 7–10). Suffice it to say here that such a view further complicates any effort at reconstructing the shape of an authentic collection.

4. Conclusion

We have mentioned three broad periods which saw editorial activity that contributed to the final form of chs. 1–39: the pre-exilic period with the prophet Isaiah himself, and possibly the supporters of Josiah; the exilic period after the destruction of Jerusalem; and the post-exilic period after the return to the land. One tangible result of such editing seen above is that the hope for return from exile and a subsequent restoration now concludes all major sections of 1–39: chs. 1–12 end with this in 11.11-16, which is concluded with a thanksgiving hymn in ch. 12; chs. 13–27 begin with this in 14.1-3 and end with it in 27.12-13 (if 24–27 is taken as an extension of the preceding oracles); chs. 28–35 end with this in ch. 35; and chs. 36–39 conclude with the announcement of exile which anticipates the restoration in 40–66. As a result, the message of Isaiah the prophet, whose name the book bears, is now seen through the lens of exile and restoration. These pivotal moments in Israel's history, now textualized, become a key part of the structure of the book.

Who were the figures that shaped the Isaianic tradition in the exilic and post-exilic periods? Many have argued that these were the very same people responsible for 40–55 and 56–66. It is to this theory in part that the next two chapters are addressed.

Chapter 2

Second-Isaiah and the Book

1. Introduction

As regards redaction more generally and the methods used to uncover it, see the introduction to the previous chapter. Here we will have a look at what scholars have said about the formation of chs. 40–55 and about how these chapters relate to chs. 1–39. As we have seen, scholars in the eighteenth century separated 40–66 from 1–39, noting that they assume the exile had already taken place, so that they could not have stemmed from the prophet Isaiah who was seen as largely responsible for the first half of the book. This view was further refined by Duhm (1892) who separated 56–66 from 40–55, arguing, among other things, that they come from a later period. While these divisions of the book have largely held their place in scholarship, the picture has become more complicated as scholars have become increasingly aware that each of these parts has played a role in the formation of the others. Many would now see 1–39 as having developed in relation to 40–66 which in turn allude to earlier material in that first part of the book.

While all of this has blurred the once ironclad boundaries between the various sections of the book, there remains a strong consensus that DI presents itself as a meaningful unit of text with its own historical setting and unique message. The exilic context to which DI addresses itself (cf. 48.20; 52.11-12) tends to distinguish it from PI, where a pre-exilic setting predominates. Moreover, while the Hezekiah narrative in 36–39 serves to introduce DI by predicting the Babylonian exile, this function clearly arose as the result of an editor juxtaposing the two blocks of material. Hence, there is a gap between the two: where ch. 39 looks forward to the Babylonian destruction of Jerusalem, DI looks back to it. No account of the destruction itself is given. The reader simply moves from a pre- to a post-destruction perspective when they cross from 39.8 ("there will be peace and truth in my [Hezekiah's] days") to 40.1-2 ("comfort, comfort my people . . . for she has received double from the hand of the Lord for all her sins"). This gap constitutes a rough edge, distinguishing what follows from what precedes. At the other end of DI after its last chapter, we find TI which assumes a later historical setting and has its own shape (see below), suggesting it ought to be distinguished from what precedes in 40–55.

If DI comes into focus as a meaningful unit of text because of what precedes and what follows it, it does so also because it has its own literary shape that marks it off. DI receives a fitting introduction in ch. 40, which begins with an announcement of the end of judgment (exile) followed by a commission to preach the good news — both of which are central to everything that follows in 40–55. For various reasons, scholars have also found ch. 55 to be a fitting conclusion for DI. Moreover, these two chapters together form a literary envelope around the whole, each stating unequivocally that God's "word" (*dbr*) will accomplish the task for which he sent it (40.8; 55.11). Scholars have cited other features (stylistic, thematic, and literary) that point to DI as a distinct unit.

This chapter of our book is concerned with two groups of questions. (1) What is the nature of DI's formation? Was it written by a single author, or does it show signs of extensive editorial handling? (2) What is the relationship of DI to the formation of the book? Was the hand(s) responsible for DI also active in editing earlier material found in PI? And, in the same vein, was the hand(s) behind TI also responsible for certain passages in DI? As we shall see, each of these questions has received more than one answer.

2. The Formation of Deutero-Isaiah

For some 20 years following Duhm's commentary, "it was still usual to regard Isa. xl-lv as a *book* written to a definite plan" (North 1964: 4). This picture began to change with Gressmann (1914) who inaugurated the form-critical study of these chapters which dominated the field up to the 1970s. For the most part, this approach viewed DI as a collection of originally *independent* literary units that reflected oral genres. For Gressmann there were 49 such units, and for those who followed him there were even more. This assessment naturally led to the view that DI is better thought of as a *collection* than as a continuous flowing composition with a "definite plan." Whether or not this collection had any overall structure or purposeful arrangement was a question largely neglected by the early form critics, and when it was addressed later on, it received varying answers (Melugin 1976: 1–10).

The aim of the form-critical approach was to study conventional forms of speech or writing. A modern example of such a form would be a letter with its relatively fixed elements: date, formal greeting ("Dear . . ."), body, concluding formula ("Sincerely,"), and signature. Form criticism was also interested in identifying the real-life settings out of which these forms arose. Another modern example in this regard would be hymns and their use in the setting of church services. When it came to DI, much of the form critics' efforts went into classifying its forms and determining the length of its literary units. Form critics generally recognized that where the prophet behind DI had employed the traditional forms of his culture, he did so with great originality, sometimes reconfiguring the forms and always reapplying them to the exilic situation in which his audience found itself.

The result of the form-critical movement was the isolation and definition of several different literary forms in DI. While no one scholar's reconstruction of these forms will agree exactly with that of another, Whybray (1983: 25–39) outlines some of the major types uncovered (cf. Melugin 1976: 13–76, Westermann 1969: 8–21). He identifies four forms employed by DI.

The first of these goes under the title "oracle of salvation," and its structure may be illustrated with 41.14-16. This passage is an ideal example in that it contains most of the features thought to belong to this form. These features are put in italics. The text begins with *the address* in v. 14a: "O worm, Jacob, O louse [emended], Israel" (cf. 41.8, 9; 43.1a; 44.1). This line also contains the *assurance of salvation*: "fear not!" This element can stand at the beginning of the address, or just after it (cf. 41.10; 43.1; 43.5; 44.2b; 54.4). This is then substantiated in v. 14b with *the basis of the assurance*: "'I am helping you,' says the Lord; 'the Holy One of Israel is your redeemer'" (cf. 41.10; 43.1, 5; 54.5). Verses 15-16a then give *the consequences of the Lord's action*, a feature usually expressed with imperfect verb forms (cf. 41.11, 12; 43.2, 5-6; 44.3-5; 54.4). Finally, the passage concludes with a statement of *the Lord's ultimate purpose* in v. 16b: "You will rejoice in the Lord; in the Holy One of Israel you will exult" (cf. 43.7; 44.5). The expression of each of these features elsewhere in DI varies from that found in 41.14-16; and not every "oracle of salvation" contains all the features listed here. In fact, Westermann divided this group into two separate forms, distinguishing between "the promise of salvation" (41.8-13, 14-16; 43.1-4, 5-7; 44.1-5) and the "proclamation of salvation" (41.17-20; 42.14-17; 43.16-21; 49.7-12). For Whybray, however, the "proclamation of salvation" is better thought of as a loose example of the "promise of salvation."

From the shape of certain psalms, many inferred that the "oracle of salvation" originally developed out of a pre-exilic rite in which persons in distress would make their appeal to the Lord at the sanctuary; the recital of that person's appeal would then be followed by an "oracle of salvation" delivered by a priest, assuring him or her that the prayer had been heard. While no "oracle of salvation" is found appended to a lament in the book of Psalms, the movement in this rite from petition to assurance was thought to explain the sudden shifts found in many psalms where the psalmist's mood changes without explanation from one of dejection to one of joy and confidence (e.g. Ps. 22.22) — the shift being caused by the priest's delivery of the oracle. Scholars have argued that the prophet responsible for DI redeployed this traditional form to address those in exile who were reciting laments at their own meetings of worship (cf. Ps. 137.1: "By the rivers of Babylon — there we sat down and wept"). This explained why many of the "oracles of salvation" in DI look like they are quoting from such laments (e.g. 49.14; 41.14, cf. Ps. 22.6).

The second form listed by Whybray is the "hymn." This form, as its label suggests, is thought to have had its origins in Israel's worship at the temple during the pre-exilic period. The first element of the "hymn" was a summons to praise the Lord that was addressed to Israel, to the peoples of the world, or to all creation. The second element recounts God's benevolence to his people, employing perfect verb forms usually in a statement about his great deeds, and often introduced by the word "for" (*ky*). Psalm 117 offers a succinct example of the "hymn":

> Praise the Lord all you nations!
>> Extol him all you peoples!
> For his mercy has prevailed over us,
>> and the truth of the Lord is forever.

There are several examples of this form in DI, revealing the prophet's dependence on Israel's liturgical tradition (cf. 42.1-13; 44.23). With Psalm 117 compare Isa. 49.13:

> Sing for joy, O heavens, and be glad, O earth;
>> Break forth, O mountains, with ringing cry!
> For the Lord has comforted his people,
>> and has compassion on his afflicted.

The parallels in theme and structure are obvious. Admitting the influence of such hymns on the oracles in DI, Westermann found a subtle distinction between two types, arguing that those represented by Psalm 117 grounded the call to praise in a statement about the Lord's *personal qualities*, whereas those represented by Isa. 49.13 grounded it in his *actions*. The latter psalm type he called an "eschatological hymn of praise," suggesting it may have been invented by the prophet behind DI (though see Exod. 15.21). According to Whybray, the older form of the "hymn" (as in Psalm 117) employed perfect verb forms to recount past actions, but the hymns in DI reused these perfect forms to impart certainty to "a future action in the making" — a usage often referred to as "the prophetic perfect."

The influence of hymns on this prophet's oracles was not limited to this form; other features of his style are also dependent on this tradition, such as, for example, his descriptions of God using participial clauses (translated with "who . . ."): "the one who created the heavens . . . who spread forth the earth . . ." (42.5, cf. Ps. 104.1-4).

Third, Whybray mentions the "trial scene," a form he finds in 41.1-5, 21-29; 43.8-13; 44.6-8+21-22 (seeing vv. 9-20 as a later interpolation); and 45.20-25. Not all of these passages exhibit each of the expected elements of the "trial scene," as it has been reconstructed. Moreover, while this form finds its structure in the scene of a trial, rarely, if ever, does it contain all of the elements of an actual trial. Whybray (1983: 36–37) cites 41.21-29 as a model example, analyzing the passage as follows:

> The language of verse 21, which sets the scene, is clearly that of the law court. Yahweh is the presiding judge, though he is also one of the parties in dispute

. . . The other side consists of the pagan gods. These are addressed and asked to present proofs of their activity and thus effectively of their existence. Verses 22-23 state the nature of the matter in dispute and the kind of evidence to be admitted. But the gods are shown by their silence to be non-existent. Yahweh then presents his own case, which is the main reason for the use of the device of the trial scene (verses 25-28) and reaches his conclusion. The concluding judgment in verse 29 is that the other so-called gods have no existence.

The trial scenes in DI have as their opponents either the gods or the nations, and their aim was not to conduct a criminal trial, but a "fact finding mission." The setting out of which such a form arose is disputed, suggestions ranging from regular court proceedings at the city gate to a trial wherein an Ancient Near Eastern king would hold a subservient party responsible for breaking the terms of a treaty between the two. Whatever the original setting of the "trial scene," it is clear that the prophet has creatively employed this form in DI as a rhetorical technique aimed at accomplishing his own goal — to convince a people reluctant to accept his message that the Lord is supreme.

The last form is the "disputation." This is frequently characterized by the argument from *analogy*, whereby the prophet begins with a fact with which his audience would agree, and proceeds to argue, on analogy with this agreed point, for something else which his audience had needed to be persuaded of. Several examples of the "disputation" arguing by analogy are found in DI (40.12-17, 18-26, 27-31; 45.9-13; 55.8-11) — though not all examples of this form adopt this logic (e.g. 46.9-11; 48.1-11, 12-16). Some have suggested the "disputation" form arose out of wisdom settings, a point rejected by Whybray who says there is no evidence for this, arguing that such forms of argument "are common to all rational speech."

In identifying and defining forms such as these, form criticism demonstrated its value as a method, but it also had its limitations. According to Whybray (1983: 24–25), there are three in particular that deserve mention. (1) Form criticism can really only be applied to forms of language that are conventional in character. And the oracles in DI reflect a prophet who frequently expressed his thoughts freely. (2) Similarly, form criticism can be applied too rigidly: "To docket every phrase in a kind of form-critical filing cabinet would be an absurd misuse of form criticism which would reveal an insensitivity to a prophet's spontaneity and creative imagination." (3) The role of form criticism in the interpretation of a passage may be limited by a prophet's use of conventional forms for his own ends, a use separating them from their original settings, by assigning them a new function. In this case, identifying the original "situation-in-life" (*Sitz im Leben*) of a form only serves to highlight the new stage of its history that it has entered through the use of the prophet — though, I would add, this may help foreground the rhetoric underlying the prophet's use of a particular form, and in this way contribute to the interpretation of its transformed use in DI.

The form critics were generally agreed that these forms were to be viewed as originally *independent* literary units reflecting oral genres, which were secondarily collected and arranged into what is now DI. Thus, DI was viewed as a *collection* of these short units. This naturally raised the question as to who collected and arranged these units into their present form in chs. 40–55, and whether or not that arrangement had any underlying logic. The hand behind this arrangement was thought to be either the prophet himself, or one of his later disciples such as the figure behind TI.

Probing the logic of the arrangement was initially overshadowed by a focus on the forms themselves, but it eventually attracted the attention of the form critics. Several views emerged. Some held that the arrangement of the pieces shows no underlying logic. Others suggested that the oracles were arranged according to the largely mechanical principles of thematic similarity and "catchword" association. Thus, it has been maintained that someone juxtaposed 45.20-25 with 46.1-4 on the basis of the verb "to bow down" (*kr*ˤ) which occurs in both, though in a different connection in each instance (45.23; 46.1).

Still others maintained that there was a deeper logic at work in the arrangement of these oracles. Melugin, who devoted a monograph to this topic, concluded that "Isaiah 40-55 . . . is a collection of originally independent units, but the arrangement is kerygmatic" (1976: 175). In other words, the hand responsible for collecting and arranging the material did so with theological intent. Hence, while Melugin would agree that a "catchword" principle was at work in the juxtaposition of 45.20-25 with 46.1-4, he also perceives a strategy underlying that juxtaposition:

> 46,1-4 continues the emphasis of chapter 45 upon the capitulation of the nations. 46,1-4 extends that theme in that these four verses do not simply promise their defeat, but give us a *picture* of their humiliated and impotent gods being carried into exile. In addition, the image of the nations left with only a residue after the defeat (45,20) is in the collection related to the epithet, "remnant of the house of Israel" in 46,3. The larger context, then, uses the image of the remnant as a means of association: a remnant of the nations confessing Yahweh before Israel (45,14-17; cf. v. 22-25), and remnant Israel (46,3), both of which inherit the new age. Ironically, the circumstances of the past and present will in the future be reversed; remnant Israel, slave of Babylon, will be served by a remnant of the nations (45,14-17) (1976: 134).

Melugin finds a further note of irony communicated through the juxtaposition of these two originally independent pieces; for, when this juxtaposition is read in the larger context, it emerges that "Israel was in exile; now the Babylonian idols which were prominently carried about (45,20) will indeed be carried — into exile!"

Melugin developed his approach in dialogue with Muilenburg (1956), an early critic of the form-critical approach who adopted instead what has been called a "rhetorical approach." Muilenburg argued that the short discrete oral forms of the pre-exilic period — to which form critics had supposed the exilic prophet was heir — had actually given way by that time to a new process of composition wherein writers were no longer bound to conventional forms. This development enabled the exilic prophet behind DI to employ these forms as he saw fit. Because he often combined several different forms when composing individual poems, it is not appropriate, Muilenburg argues, to use these forms as a basis for isolating originally independent units. These lengthy poems were constructed by means of stanzas or strophes, such that one could detect a progression of thought in chs. 40–55. While subsequent form critics such as Melugin were able to incorporate many of Muilenburg's insights, they nevertheless felt that he had rather down played the role of traditional speech forms in DI, which for them remained a significant aspect of the material.

All three conclusions — that the arrangement shows no logic, that it is purely mechanical, and that it reflects a meaningful strategy — are reached on the basis of a prior form-critical analysis of the units themselves (except, of course, in the case of Muilenburg who took a different approach). The number of such units and their proper delimitation are very much a matter of debate, so that differing results in the initial form-critical analysis have inevitably led to differing assessments of the nature of the collection.

Like their predecessors, form critics agreed that the material in 40–55 stemmed from a single prophet working in the exilic period, though there were two major exceptions to this: (1) the four so-called "servant songs" (42.1-4; 49.1-6; 50.4-11; 52.13–53.12) and (2) certain passages containing idol polemic (especially 40.19-20; 41.5-7; 44.9-20), both of which were initially isolated by Duhm as later additions to the text. While this view was widely adopted for both sets of passages, several more recent studies have challenged it, arguing that these texts are far more integrated into their contexts than was previously recognized (e.g. Clifford 1980, Mettinger 1983).

To take one example from the "servant songs," we may note that 42.1-4 (which was considered secondary) is clearly related to 41.8-10 (which was not). In both, one finds reference made to the "servant" and "chosen one" whom God will "uphold" (*tmk*) — a verb occurring only one further time in the book where the connection is quite different (33.15). This close connection suggests that 42.1-4 is not part of an unrelated stratum secondarily inserted into its present context. Of course, we could explain this close relationship while continuing to maintain that 42.1-4 is a secondary addition, as long as we concede that this passage was written-up in the light of its context (i.e. 41.8-10). Thus, it would be secondary, but compositionally related to its context. But the more one finds that these "songs" are related to their contexts, the less compelling Duhm's argument appears: this finding undermines the very reason for their isolation in the first place — a loose relation to their contexts.

Naturally this whole debate has had important implications for interpreting the "servant songs," in particular, for identifying the servant mentioned in them. This identification has been much debated, some of the more common proposals being: Israel, Cyrus, a prophet, or a royal figure. Moreover, do all of the "songs" have the same referent, or do different ones speak of different figures (whether corporate or individual)? The older approach initiated by Duhm tended to go about answering this without much reference to the context of these "songs," since they were seen as later additions that essentially constituted a separate literary stratum. That move opened the door to a whole variety of identifications, freeing these "songs" from their respective contexts in DI where Israel is frequently referred to as the "servant." One example of this is 41.8 which is clearly related to 42.1, as was just noted.

However, if these "songs" are not secondary, then appeal to context is essential in defining the identity of the servant. One attempt to interpret these "songs" in context is offered by Wilcox and Paton-Williams (1988) who seek to illuminate the identity of the servant with an eye toward the widely recognized transition from the first section of DI (40–48) to the second (49–55). When the "servant songs" are read in context and in the light of this shift in DI, the following pattern emerges:

1. In chs. 40-48 the servant is Israel. The prophet has a mission to Israel; Israel has a mission to the nations. But servant Israel's sufferings, though fully deserved and now ended, have left him despondent and unable to fulfill his calling.
2. In chs. 49-55 the servant is the prophet. The prophet has a double mission now, both to Israel and to the nations. The servant prophet accepts his sufferings, and fulfils his mission initially despite them (49.1-6; 50.4-9), and ultimately because of them (52.13-53.12) (1988: 98–99).

For Wilcox and Paton-Williams, such an interpretation explains several features of the "songs," not least the oddity of 49.1-6 wherein v. 3 identifies the servant *as Israel*, but v. 5 gives the servant a mission *to Israel*, a clear reference to a prophetic figure. They argue that this contradiction (which some try to solve by emending the text despite the lack of textual evidence for this) is only apparent, since it is the prophet who is called Israel in v. 3. In 40–48 Israel is called servant and has a mission to the nations; this is transferred to the prophet in 49.5-6: "in effect, by the redefinition of his mission to include the nations, and by his designation as 'servant of the LORD,' the prophet has become [the true] Israel" (Wilcox and Paton-Williams 1988: 92). Thus, in v. 3 the word "Israel" is not a vocative ("You are my servant, [O] Israel") but "a predicate, parallel to 'servant' ('You are my servant, [you are] Israel')." This interpretation explains a number of differences between 40–48 and 49–55 that Wilcox and Paton-Williams outline. For example, in 40–48 the servant is explicitly called Israel, whereas in 49–55 this is never the case (except in 49.3 where the reader witnesses a transference taking place).

Whether or not such a reading is correct, it does illustrate the point that some recent studies have moved away from Duhm's separation of the so-called "servant songs" from their context, and that this move has had significant ramifications for interpreting these passages.

Thus, while Duhm (and the many that followed him) saw these two sets of passages as secondary to DI, there has been a noticeable trend in the opposite direction, a trend toward regarding these texts as having stemmed from the exilic prophet. As a result, it is no longer axiomatic to treat as secondary the "servant songs" and the idol-satire passages. This trend has only strengthened the older consensus which saw most of 40–55 as coming from the hand of a single prophet. This consensus was supported by Duhm and his followers, despite their excising the two sets of passages just noted; it was supported by the form critics; and it continues to find support in many recent commentaries which still find DI largely coherent, and see much of the material there as stemming from a single prophet (see Williamson 2009: 35 nt. 47).

This picture contrasts sharply with many recent studies in German detecting several pervasive levels of redaction in DI. These studies have been steadily gaining momentum since the 1970s, and (if accepted) tend to undermine the view just described, that DI essentially conveys the thought of a single mind. They find significantly more redactional intervention in DI than the older view, going far beyond the judgment that the "servant songs" and idol-polemic passages are later insertions. At the same time, the redactional models advanced by these newer studies differ substantially from one another — some, for example, finding the original core of material only in 40–46, while others uncovering it in every chapter from 40 to 55. This core was then subjected to any number of a variety of redactional additions whose nature and extent depend on which model is in view.

In a recent survey of these diverse proposals, Albertz (2004: 376–434) seeks to identify those points at which their conclusions overlap, and then to build on these in developing his own model. In many of these models, Albertz finds two problems that he seeks to remedy in his approach: (1) some of the proposals assign the "eschatological hymns" (42.10-13; 44.23; 45.8; 48.20-21; 49.13; 52.9-10) to more than one level of redaction, a move he finds implausible since these serve an important structural function that suggests a single hand; (2) some of these models fail to reckon with 52.7-12 which he regards as a clear conclusion to an earlier edition now incorporated into the present form of DI.

The latter position serves as the starting point for Albertz's analysis. Building on his survey of approaches, he argues that DI in its present form possesses two conclusions, one in 52.7-12 and the other in 55.6, 8-13. From this he draws the conclusion that DI went through two editions (minor additions aside). Moreover, each of these book conclusions was matched by introductory material in the first chapter of DI. Isaiah 52.7-12 was matched by 40.1-5*, 9-11 — both speaking of "comfort" and the "herald of good news." Isaiah 55.6, 8-13 was paired with 40.6-8* — both "emphasizing the power and endurance of God's word." Using these two book conclusions as his points of reference, Albertz proceeds to work out two editions of DI. The first of these spans 40.1–52.12*, and the second 40.1–55.13. While the second edition added a new conclusion to the first, it also inserted much new material within it, reshaping the whole. The first edition was structured by means of the "eschatological hymns," which is why, according to Albertz, these hymns are not found after 52.12 — the last verse of that edition.

As for the date of each edition, Albertz assigns the first to the year 521 B.C.E. when the Persian king Darius was in power, despite the fact that DI only mentions Cyrus (a king who preceded Darius). While Albertz finds it much more difficult to date the second edition of DI, he concludes that, since it is presupposed by the earliest core of TI (chs. 60–62) which dates from the first half of the fifth century at the latest, it must stem from sometime before that (though of course after the first edition was completed).

Albertz's analysis involves far more detail than can be given here. We may note, however, that his conclusions seem more moderate than those reached by some of the approaches he surveys. Only time will tell just how successful Albertz is in his effort to draw together the common conclusions of these multifarious proposals for the purpose of setting forth a new model aimed at finding general acceptance.

3. Deutero-Isaiah and the Formation of the Book

As we noted in the introduction to this chapter, Isaiah 40–55 was seen for a very long time as having developed independently from 1–39. Scholars thought DI had been appended to PI only at a very late date after both sections had more or less reached their present forms. This whole view has now been called into question. Many scholars now argue that DI is actually highly indebted to earlier passages in PI for its outlook and diction, suggesting that at the outset it was written as a direct literary continuation of these older passages.

To take perhaps the best known example of this, Isaiah 6 is widely regarded as having had considerable influence on the oracles in DI (cf. Uhlig 2009). DI alludes to this chapter time and again in drawing up its own message. It will be recalled that the majority of scholars regard at least part of ch. 6 as having been written in the pre-exilic period, so that this part of the book will have been in place well before the writing of DI.

One much noted instance of influence from ch. 6 comes from vv. 9-10, the task for which Isaiah was commissioned:

> Go, say to this people:
> 'Hearing, hear, but do not understand;
>   seeing, see, but do not perceive."
> Make the heart of this people fat,
>   their ears heavy,
>   and shut their eyes;
> lest they see with their eyes,
>   and hear with their ears,
> and understand with their heart,
>   and turn and be healed.

This passage is taken up at several points in DI, in particular, by those passages drawing from the cluster of terms found here ("see" [$r\ˀh$], "hear" [*šm*ʿ], "understand" [*byn*], "know/perceive" [*ydʿ*]). See, for example, 42.18-19; 43.8; 44.18-19. This cluster of terms is distinctively Isaianic. Isaiah 41.20 offers one example of influence. In context, this passage describes the intended consequences of God's new salvation. He would act on behalf of his people "so that they *may see and know* . . . that the hand of the Lord has done this and the Holy One of Israel has created it." Here one witnesses a reversal of the judgment in 6.9-10 where the people were told "seeing, see, but do not know." Once impaired, spiritual perception would now be renewed. We might also note that 41.20 employs the divine title "Holy One of Israel," a title many regard as having been drawn from passages attributable to Isaiah himself (e.g. 1.4; 5.19, 24; 30.11, 12, 15; 31.1). The use of this divine title may have been encouraged by the vision in ch. 6 where the seraphim proclaim "Holy, holy, holy is the Lord of Hosts" (v. 3).

Another widely recognized example of the influence of ch. 6 comes in 40.1-8 where scholars have long detected the elements of a heavenly court scene, the precise setting of the earlier passage. Besides this, the two texts share several other features in common:

> in both there is a reference to 'a voice calling' (*qôl qôrēʾ*) (6:4; 40:3) and then to 'a voice speaking' (*qôl ʾōmēr*) (6:8; 40:6); both the usage, and certainly the combination, appear to be unparalleled elsewhere. In both the prophet responds with initial despair (6:5; 40:6); in both there is reference to the removal of sin and iniquity (*ḥṭ'ṭ* and *ʿwn* (6:7; 40:2; cf. 1:4)); and in both there is an emphasis on the glory (*kbwd*) of God (6:3; 40:5) (Williamson 1994: 38).

As Williamson recognizes, there are some important differences in the ways in which these various elements are used in each passage, so that it is clear that the later author has used the earlier passage in development.

One interpretation of this is offered by Seitz (1990) who argues that 40.1-11 signals the end of the old age of judgment spoken of in 6.11-12, ushering in a new age: "It is time for the herald of good tidings to replace the voices of past guilt and former judgment" (1990: 243). At the same time, underlying this transition was an abiding sense of theological continuity, since the reference also evokes the commission in ch. 6: "Ackroyd is finally correct that 40:1-11 is a 'renewal of the Isaianic commission,' not because Isaiah is recommissioned, but because God speaks again from the divine council as he had done formerly in Isaiah's day" (1990: 245). Irrespective of the validity of this (sensitive) reading, the point remains that earlier passages in PI were taken up through allusion in DI.

While such literary influence was certainly not limited to earlier passages from PI (cf. Nurmela 2006), many would regard this earlier material as having had a particularly strong influence on DI, and that to such a degree that it should no longer be regarded as having developed independently from some form of the first half of the book. Accordingly, many now regard DI as a direct literary continuation of some earlier form of PI. For them, DI never existed as an independent work.

This in turn has raised the question as to whether the individual(s) behind DI might not have had a role in editing some form of PI. If they were so influenced by this earlier collection, and if they added to it their own work in the form of chs. 40–55, then it is only a small step to suggest that they may have intervened more directly in that collection through editing.

This view has been advanced most forcefully by Williamson (1994) whose argument accepted what was then still the consensus view of DI's authorship, that most of it stems from a single individual whom scholars have called "Deutero-Isaiah." This view is still upheld by many, but has also been challenged by recent developments in redaction critical work on these chapters (see above). Outlining the main conclusions of his study, Williamson writes,

> I have argued for three main proposals in the course of this book, namely (i) that Deutero-Isaiah was especially influenced by the literary deposit of Isaiah of Jerusalem . . . (ii) that he regarded the earlier work as in some sense a book that had been sealed up until the time when judgement should be passed and the day of salvation had arrived, which day he believed himself to be heralding . . . and (iii) that in order to locate his message in relation to the earlier and continuing ways of God with Israel he included a version of the earlier prophecies with his own and edited them in such a way as to bind the two parts of the work together (1994: 240–241).

Far from seeing DI as an independent work, therefore, Williamson believes that it was written in conscious dependence on some form of PI, and that in turn PI was edited with a view toward DI. In this way, Isaiah 1–55, though containing pre-exilic material, was actually an exilic work (excepting of course various additions and rearrangements that had taken place in the even later post-exilic period).

As we have seen, several studies have supported the first point: "that Deutero-Isaiah was especially influenced by the literary deposit of Isaiah of Jerusalem." The second point seeks to provide some rationale as to why the prophet would have been interested in this editorial task to begin with. The third point is clearly what the rest of the book is building toward: Deutero-Isaiah as editor of the Isaianic deposit.

Taking one example from this third leg of the argument, we note that Williamson (1994: 116–155) regards 11.11-16 and 12.1-6 as Deutero-Isaianic compositions written up for their present location in 1–39. To begin with, the form and function of the psalm in 12.1-6 are characteristic of DI's "eschatological hymns of praise," as described by Westermann and widely accepted by subsequent scholarship (on these see pp. 29–30 above). As in these hymns, the praise in 12.1-6 relates to future events, while its substantiation is put in the past tense. These hymns are also thought to play a major structural role in DI, precisely the function many would assign to 12.1-6 within PI.

Moreover, the major themes in the psalm correspond with those of DI, sometimes being cast in the same vocabulary. The psalm speaks of a period of God's anger (v. 1) like DI (e.g. 42.25; 48.9); it then switches to

SECOND-ISAIAH AND THE BOOK 39

the experience of salvation and accompanying joy (vv. 1c-3, 6), expressing this with language that is characteristic of DI ("you did comfort me"
[nhm], e.g. 40.1; 49.13; 51.3, 12, 19; "salvation" [yᵉšûᵃ], e.g. 49.6, 8;
51.6, 8); and it concludes with a call to praise and proclaim this to the
nations who are also summoned to rejoice (vv. 4-6), the psalm again using
phrases characteristic of this later part of the book (cf. 42.10; 48.20; 54.1).
In addition, the psalm evokes the first exodus for this new time of salvation
(v. 2, 5; cf. Exod. 15.1-2) — a move also made by DI, as has long been
recognized (e.g. 41.17-18; 43.19-20). In the light of these considerations,
Williamson concludes that 12.1-6 was likely written by Deutero-Isaiah
who placed it in its present position.

Because the psalm in 12.1-6 clearly relates itself to the preceding
passage in 11.11-16 (note the theme of a second exodus in both, for
example), Williamson considers whether or not a similar conclusion
might be appropriate for this passage as well. Isaiah 11.11-16 is widely
regarded as post-Isaianic, having been written no earlier than the exile.
Taking this as his starting point, he proceeds to build a case for Deutero-
Isaianic authorship of this passage. To this end, he draws attention to the
many points at which 11.11-16 reflects the thought and diction of DI. For
example, both 11.12 and 49.22 refer to God raising a "signal" (nēs) to
the nations to "regather" (qbṣ) the Israelite diaspora (this verb commonly
expresses return in DI: 40.11; 43.5; 49.18; 54.7). Isaiah 11.16; 40.3; 49.11
all speak of a "highway" (mslh) upon which the exiles are to return. And
Isaiah 11.15-16, like DI generally, depicts return from exile in terms of
the Exodus from Egypt (e.g. drying of the sea in 11.15; 50.2; 51.10; and
returning on dry ground in 11.15; 42.15; 43.16; 44.27; 51.10). On the
basis of such parallels as well as other considerations, Williamson argues
that 11.11-16 stems from Deutero-Isaiah. His assessment of this passage
is bound up with his analysis of 5.25-30 which shares the phrase "raise a
signal to the nations" with 11.12, and is widely thought to owe its present
position to editorial rearrangement.

Williamson uncovers several passages like these throughout chs. 1–39,
passages which on the one hand are patently editorial, and on the other
reflect distinctive aspects of DI's language and theology. From all of this
there emerges a cumulative case for Deutero-Isaiah as an editor of the
earlier Isaianic deposit, a case that must at least be considered a "plausible
hypothesis," to use Williamson's phrase. In comparison with much recent
redaction critical work on Isaiah, this hypothesis has the advantage of
simplicity, providing an elegant explanation for a whole series of passages
in PI, while avoiding the danger facing some theories of collapsing under
the weight of their own complexity.

Efforts to illuminate the relationship between DI and PI (such as
Williamson's) are now not uncommon, since these two parts of the book
are no longer widely held to have developed independently from one
another. And since PI passed through a stage of editing in the exilic period
(as was seen above), it makes sense to consider the possibility that such
editing might have been undertaken in conjunction with the formation
of DI which also stems from this period.

4. Conclusion

This discussion has shown that there are now competing ideas about the formation of DI, some arguing that it is largely coherent and stems mainly from a single figure, while others asserting that it is the product of multiple redactions. This discussion has also shown that the formation of DI is now being considered in relation to PI, and vice versa. Some would argue that DI looks back to PI in allusion, and that PI was edited with a view toward DI. The effect of all of this on the meaning of the book will be considered briefly at the end of the next chapter, and more fully in the chapters following that.

Chapter 3

Third-Isaiah and the Book

1. Introduction

As with DI, we need to consider two questions concerning TI: (1) What is the nature of TI's formation? (2) What is the relationship between TI and the formation of the book as a whole? But first we should briefly consider the reasons why TI is regarded as a literary block distinct from DI, a distinction first proposed by Duhm, and accepted by most scholars since (though see those mentioned by Middlemas 2005: 164 nt. 1).

Several features of TI distinguish it from DI, the first being its literary shape. TI has a shape unto itself, beginning and ending with passages which echo one another, so that the whole is placed within a sort of literary frame. This frame has long been recognized, and is made up of chs. 56.1-8 and chs. 65–66, two passages which employ the same language to depict a similar scenario involving the nations and a return to God's "holy mountain." This literary envelope around TI will be discussed below. Suffice it to say here that this envelope gives TI a distinct structure, thereby distinguishing it from DI which stands outside of that structure.

TI is further distinguished from what precedes it by 56.1, its opening verse. As Rendtorff (1993) has shown, 56.1 clearly marks the beginning of something new with respect to the book as a whole, a point emerging from this verse's handling of "righteousness" (*ṣedeq/ṣᵉdāqâ*). Where PI pairs "righteousness" with the word "judgment" (*mišpāṭ*) several times, DI never does. Instead, DI frequently associates it with words from the root *yšᶜ* ("salvation, to save", etc.) — an association not found in PI. In this way, the word is made to emphasize human righteousness in the first part of the book, but divine salvation in the second. In 56.1, however, these two usages are drawn together:

Keep judgment (*mišpāṭ*) and do righteousness (*ṣᵉdāqâ*);
    For my salvation (*yᵉšûᶜâ*) is near to come, and my righteousness (*ṣᵉdāqâ*) to be revealed.

In Isaiah, this combination does not occur before 56.1, suggesting to Rendtorff that this verse was to mark a new beginning in the book. If so, then this would further distinguish TI from DI.

Besides TI's literary shape, there are two further aspects of this material that separate it from what precedes. The first is its date. Where DI looks forward to the role of Cyrus in rebuilding the Jewish temple (chs. 44–45), TI seems to assume that that temple is already built, or that its building is already under way (56.1-8; 66.1, 20). The second feature distinguishing TI is its reuse of material from DI through allusion. These allusions often develop the earlier passages in new ways, suggesting that TI was written by a different author, one who approached DI as a reader. This much is implied in Rendorff's analysis of 56.1 just mentioned, and will be further elaborated on below. For these reasons and others, scholars have rightly distinguished TI as a distinct literary unit in the book.

2. The Formation of Third-Isaiah

In contrast to DI, which in the past has largely been viewed as a coherent work stemming from a single figure (though this is now being challenged as we saw), TI has long been regarded as a composite piece made up of sources and later additions. While Duhm thought TI stemmed more or less from a single author, most now agree that it is the product of several hands, and this despite the attempt of Elliger (1928) to support the earlier position of unity. If it can be said that most scholars now regard this work as composite, it should be noted that they disagree over how this is the case, some viewing TI as a complex web of redactional layers (e.g. Koenen 1990), while others seeing in it a single source surrounded by later compositions which are largely unified and quite extensive (e.g. Smith 1995). The former group takes a predominantly fissive approach to the material, while the latter finds more unity.

Despite this disagreement, two points have emerged that seem to be widely held. The first is that the earliest material comes in chs. 60–62, a core around which most of the rest of TI was later added. Whether or not 60–62 belong to an early layer that can be found throughout TI is a matter of some debate. Answers to this tend to be divided along the lines of the two groups just noted. The more fissive approach regards 60–62 as belonging to an early layer found throughout TI. In contrast, those finding more unity in TI do not find a pervasive layer associated with 60–62; for them, this core constitutes a source unto itself. The second point widely held is that 56.1-8 and 65–66 together form a late frame around the whole, and were written (or assembled) by the hand responsible for the final form of TI. Our survey will take these two areas of agreement in turn, and then see what might be said about the rest of TI. The following discussion draws on my own account of this problem (Stromberg 2010: 11–30).

We may begin with the vision of Jerusalem's restoration in 60–62 where the city enjoys the wealth and attention of the nations attracted to it when the divine glory appears there. Scholars are in broad agreement that these chapters form the earliest core of TI, a nucleus around which much of the rest of TI was later added in deliberate development of it. Several factors have led to this conclusion, only a few of which can be mentioned here.

This core reflects such sharp differences in outlook from what surrounds it (especially 56–59 and 65–66) that attribution of both to a single author seems implausible. Emmerson (1992: 55) writes,

> The stern denunciation of the community's leaders (56.9-12), the description of illicit religious practices rife within the community (57.1-13; 65.1-7), and the accusation that their religious observances are simply a matter of ritual without regard to social obligation (ch. 58) all stand awkwardly alongside the unconditional promises in chs. 60-62. It is difficult also to relate these promises, which are addressed to the entire community, to the situation of tension and outright opposition between hostile factions which is the background of 65.8-16 and 66.5.

These and other differences in outlook are accompanied by differences in style and vocabulary. For example, while divine speech formulae abound in 56–59 and 65–66 (e.g. "thus says the Lord"), these never occur in 60–62. Since their absence in these chapters does not appear to serve any particular function, this tends to strengthen the view that a separate hand is at work here.

Concluding therefore that the vision of 60–62 differs in terms of authorship from much of the material around it, we should quickly add that much of that surrounding material has been written in conscious development of it. Most scholars would agree that the vision in 60–62 has been developed by 56–59 and 65–66. One example of this comes in 58–59, chapters widely recognized as alluding to this earlier vision. These chapters take up and qualify the imminent and unconditional promise of salvation in 60–62. In 60–62, the people are promised that God will remove the present time of darkness (ḥšk), causing his glory (kbwd) to shine over Jerusalem as a bright light ('wr), and bringing righteousness (ṣdq) (see especially 60.1-3, 19-20; 62.2). Chapters 58–59 seek to respond to doubts that had arisen over whether or not this vision could actually be fulfilled. This of course implies that 58–59 were written some time after this vision was given, long enough at least for doubt to set in (cf. 59.1). To such doubt, 59.9 offers an alternative explanation, taking up the key terms of the vision of 60–62.

> For this reason [i.e. sin] justice is far from us and righteousness (ṣdqh) has not overtaken us, we expect light ('wr) but behold, darkness (ḥšk), brightness, but in gloom we walk about.

According to this verse, the vision in 60–62 remained unfulfilled, not because God was unable to bring it to fruition (a doubt to which 59.1 clearly responds: "the hand of the Lord is *not* too short to save"). Rather, it remained unfulfilled because of the people's sins, which are described in the preceding verses (vv. 1-8). The notion of a delay due to sin is found nowhere in 60–62.

How then could the people receive the promises described in 60–62? The answer comes in ch. 58, another passage that develops this early core. According to 58.6-10, the vision would be fulfilled only after they ceased their sinful ways: "If you remove the yoke from your midst . . . then your light (ʾwr) will shine in the darkness (ḥšk) and your gloom will be like noonday" (vv. 9-10). It would be fulfilled when they started doing good:

> When you see someone naked and you cover him and you do not hide yourself from your relative, then your light (ʾwr) will break forth like the dawn, and your healing will quickly sprout up, and your deliverance (ṣdq) will go before you and the glory (kbwd) of the Lord will gather you. (58.7-8)

Thus, what was promised unconditionally in 60–62 is now seen by 58–59 to depend on the people's behavior. This further illustrates the point that 60–62 as an earlier core is presupposed and developed in new directions by the outer-lying material in TI, directions no doubt necessitated by changed circumstances.

In light of this and the fact that 60–62 are heavily dependent on 40–55, many scholars date this core material later than the composition of DI, but earlier than the bulk of the remaining material in TI.

While scholars have identified 60–62 as the earliest part of TI, they regard 56.1-8 and 65–66 as its latest, these passages forming a literary frame around the whole. Despite debate over whether these passages are original compositions or redactional assemblages, scholars are generally agreed that this frame stems from the hand responsible for TI's final form.

In support of this, scholars note several parallels which bind these two passages together. (1) Both passages speak of an eschatological movement toward "my holy mountain" (56.7; 66.19-20). (2) In both, this movement culminates in an inclusive attitude toward foreigners with respect to the cult. They would have access to the temple (56.7; 66.21 by implication), and apparently even its priesthood. The latter point is probably implied by the expression translated "to serve the Lord" in 56.6, and by the promise in 66.21: "I will also take some of them [the nations] to be Levitical Priests." (3) Both passages develop this scenario through the promise to "gather" (qbṣ) the nations (56.8; 66.18). (4) Both place special emphasis on keeping the Sabbath, an emphasis that falls on non-Israelites (56.2, 4, 6; 66.23). (5) Both employ identical language to describe obedience. The righteous "choose that which I desire" (56.4); and the wicked "chose that which I did not desire" (65.12; 66.4). (6) Both passages call the obedient the "servants" of the Lord (56.6; 65.8-9, 13-15; 66.14). (7) In both, a "name" is promised to the obedient (56.5; 65.15). While other parallels could be added, these are sufficient to show that 56.1-8 and 65–66 were composed (or assembled) to form a frame around the whole of TI. Since this suggests that the frame's author had the whole of TI in front of him, it follows that he was likely the final redactor of this part of the book of Isaiah.

That this frame is, at any rate, later than the core discussed above (chs. 60–62) is evident from allusions in the former to the latter. Like 58–59, the frame develops 60–62. Thus, many have argued that this is so in 56.6. When this verse speaks of the foreigner (*bny hnkr*) who would serve (*šrt*) the Lord, there seems to be a clear development of 61.5-6 which promises that the foreigner (*bny nkr*) would serve the Israelites who are called "servants (*šrt*) of our God." Another instance of probable development comes in 56.7. When this verse promises that the offerings of the obedient foreigner will be acceptable (*rṣwn*) upon "my altar" (*mzbḥ*), it probably develops 60.7 where it is said that the flocks of foreign nations will be gathered to serve Zion, ascending with acceptance (*rṣwn*) upon "my altar" (*mzbḥ*). In both instances of allusion, the later passage develops the earlier by giving foreigners direct access to the worship of God, as if they were Israelites themselves.

The other end of this frame (chs. 65–66) also develops 60–62. To cite only one example, when 66.11 comforts those who mourn over Zion with the words, "you will suckle and be satisfied from the breast of her [Jerusalem's] comforts," it takes up 60.16 which promises Zion, "you will suckle the milk of nations, and the breast of kings you will suckle." In addition to reconfiguring the odd image of breastfeeding kings, 66.11 reapplies to individuals the address originally made to Zion. Moreover, these individuals are seen in the context to be the righteous ones who are contrasted with the wicked (e.g. 66.5, 14). No such distinction is made in 60–62. By means of this textual reapplication, the restoration initially promised to the whole in 60–62 is now limited to a few.

In light of examples such as these, scholars have reasonably concluded that the frame of TI is later than its core, adding further support to the view that this frame stems from the final editor.

As I noted above, there is some disagreement over whether this frame is an original composition or a redactional assemblage. Were 56.1-8 and 65–66 written from scratch, or were they "put together" from pre-existing sources? While some would claim that 56.1-8 shows signs of having been edited, it is more probable that this short passage was composed without the use of any sources. It flows quite nicely and does not exhibit any of real tension within itself.

While the same can be argued for 65–66, the case is admittedly less certain, not least due to the length and complexity of these chapters. The most serious challenge to the compositional unity of these chapters issues from the commentary of Westermann (1969) who found two earlier sources embedded in this material, sources which sprung from the same hand that wrote the earlier core in 60–62. These sources come in 65.16b-25 and 66.6-16, both of which show substantial overlap with the message and vocabulary of 60–62.

Although Westermann's view has been very influential on later redaction-critical treatments of these chapters, it has been challenged by Smith (1995: 144–148, 160–162) who argues that the links between these two passages and 60–62 arise from dependence rather than common authorship. In other words, 65.16b-25 and 66.6-16 look back in dependence on an earlier 60–62, developing this material. One example of this was already cited above (i.e. 66.11 as an allusion to 60.16). While I find Smith's analysis convincing, there remains room for debate here, as in most other redactional analyses.

Having now seen that scholars regard 60–62 as the earliest material, and 56.1-8 and 65–66 as the latest, we may now move on to the rest of TI and ask how it relates to one or the other of these two blocks of material.

To begin with the lament in 63.7–64.12, we may note that there is widespread agreement that 65–66 presuppose this poem, responding to it in a critical, yet attentive manner. Hence, where 64.11 complains that "our holy house [i.e. temple] . . . has been burnt with fire," 66.1 has God responding, "the heavens are my throne and the earth my footstool; where is the house you will build for me?" And where 63.17 pleads "return on account of your servants" (the servants being "all of us" [64.6, 9]), 65.8 responds "I will act on account of my servants, so as not to destroy all." The phrase "on account of" + "servants" is found nowhere else in the OT besides these two verses. The lament assumes that "all" are "your servants", but the reply limits the "servants" to a righteous group within the "all." Judgment was coming, but not all would perish. His servants would remain. The reply is thus attentive to the request, but critical of its underlying assumption. Further examples where 65–66 respond to this lament in development could be given. On the basis of such examples, many have concluded that 63.7–64.12 is an earlier source that has been incorporated into TI, probably by the hand responsible for 65–66. In support of this conclusion, I would note that in the first example, 64.11 asserts that the temple remained in ruins, whereas 66.1 appears to assume that its construction was underway, or about to be undertaken, or was already finished — any one of which suggests that the situation had developed beyond that assumed by 64.11.

Next we may consider 56.9–59.21, where the debate is over whether this constitutes an editorial assemblage of some sort, or a series of long poems composed more or less from scratch. In support of the latter, Smith (1995: 67–127) argues that this material constitutes two coherent poems (56.9–57.21; 58.1–59.20), each exhibiting rhetorical and stylistic features, such as "the use of key words, repetition, polysemy, concentric structures, and antitheses" (1995: 96). Since these features interlace each poem, it becomes difficult to break up this material into smaller fragments and redactions (though he does regard 59.21 as a later addition). Other scholars have also found more unity in this material than the fragmentary approaches allow.

While the fragmentary approaches differ considerably from one another in construing the material, many of them have in common that they find fragments of an earlier source embedded in it. The nature and extent of these fragments are debated; however one passage usually gets identified by these studies as a fragment stemming from the hand responsible for 60–62, and that is 57.14-20*, which has some points in common with this core (compare, for example, 57.14 with 62.10). However, to view this passage as an earlier source from this hand requires removing certain parts of it on the basis that they are later additions, one example being v. 21 ("there is no peace for the wicked, says my God"). This is removed, because the division it implies — one between the righteous and the wicked — fails to appear in 60–62. But since v. 22 also speaks of the "wicked" others would remove this verse as well (though it forms a nice contrast with v. 21). Even allowing for the removal of these verses, one is still left with v. 14 which speaks of a "stumbling block" in the way of the people that needs to be removed before salvation can come. This suggests some form of iniquity, such as that described in what immediately precedes this passage (vv. 3-13). It also suggests that the salvation was being delayed by this. Neither of these thoughts is found in 60–62. Moreover, there are clear lines of continuity between 57.14-21 and the frame of TI (compare, for example, 57.15 and 66.2).

Whether or not Smith's case for the unity of 56.9–59.20 ultimately convinces, this material (at least in its final form) should probably be dated later than 60–62, since it alludes to this early core in development, a point seen above in connection with 58–59. Supporting this relative dating, Smith also argues that the two poems (56.9–57.21; 58.1–59.20) are bound too closely with material in 56.1-8 and 65–66 to be separated from this frame and assigned to an earlier layer. These poems and the frame exhibit inter-connections of style, vocabulary, and outlook, indicating common authorship rather than development of one author's work by another.

In sum, certain trends are evident in the redaction-critical treatment of 56.9–59.21, though many views of the formation of this material have been set forth. It goes without saying that the few comments made here can hardly be expected to settle the matter.

The last passage to be considered comes in 63.1-7, an oracle against Edom and the nations. It is widely recognized that this passage, together with 59.15-20, serves to frame 60–62. In both passages, God appears as a mighty warrior ready to act in salvation and judgment. The points of contact are especially evident in the following verses which recount the reasons for the divine action.

> I looked, but there was none to help;
>> and I was amazed, but there was none to uphold;
> so my own arm worked salvation for me,
>> and my wrath upheld me. (63.5)

> He saw that there was no one,
>> and he was amazed that there was none to intercede;
> so his own arm worked salvation for him,
>> and his righteousness upheld him. (59.16)

In addition to this very close parallel, 59.15-20 and 63.1-7 both describe God's clothing and speak of his coming "vengeance." Scholars explain the relationship between these two passages in one of three ways: (1) both were written by the same hand; (2) 63.1-7 was written later than, and is dependent on, 59.15-20; or (3) the reverse, so that 59.15-20 is the later of the two.

My own study (referred to above) follows those who argue for option (3) — that 59.15-20 is later. In support of this, it may be observed that 63.5 exhibits a number of subtle poetic features which appear to be disrupted in 59.16 by elements drawn from the context of that verse (e.g. the replacement of "wrath" with "righteousness" under the influence of v. 14). In this light, 59.16 looks like a quotation of 63.5 that adapts its content to the new context. If this is correct, it would explain other differences as well. Isaiah 63.1-6 depicts God wearing clothing stained with grape juice (i.e. the blood of the enemies). This image is transformed in 59.15-20: here God clothes himself with righteousness, salvation, vengeance, and zeal. Thus, the image shifts from the concrete to the abstract. It also appears as if 63.1-7 has been reinterpreted in terms of the intra-community division present in 56–59 and 65–66. For, where 63.1-7 applies the judgment only to foreign nations, 59.15-20 applies this to the Israelite community (cf. vv. 9-14, 20). Since this reinterpretation mirrors that of 60–62 as they are taken up in the frame of TI, some have reasonably concluded that 59.15-20 stems from the same author as that frame. It will be recalled that Smith arrives at the same conclusion, but for different reasons.

Whether TI is to be thought of as highly fragmented, or as a more unified composition, many would agree that its present form is roughly symmetrical. Working outward from the central panel in 60–62, Blenkinsopp (2003: 39) describes this symmetry as follows:

> YHVH is presented as warrior and vindicator of his people immediately before and after this central panel (59:15b-20; 63:1-6). There are laments, or at least complaints, before and after it (59:1-15a; 63:7-64:11); the former lament receives a positive response (59:15b-20), while the latter is given only an explanation why a positive response is not forthcoming (65:1-7). The denunciation of heterodox cult practices in 57:3-13 and 65:1-7 could also be seen as roughly symmetrical. Several scholars, finally, are convinced that 56:1-8 and 66:18-24 form an inclusio for the text as a whole.

While there is always a danger in finding parallel structures where none exist (as Blenkinsopp recognizes), this sketch does seem to suggest an attempt on the part of a redactor to give the material some sort of meaningful shape.

3. Third-Isaiah and the Formation of the Book

What is the relationship between TI and the formation of the book as a whole? This question is receiving increased attention from those scholars interested in the formation of the book, and this for at least two reasons. First, while scholars have long treated 40–66 separately from 1–39 when it comes to composition, it has become clear that this later part of the book was written with the knowledge of some form of the earlier part. This is especially true for TI; several studies have shown the dependence of this part of the book on earlier Isaianic material (see those mentioned in Nurmela 2006). The second reason scholars are now giving attention to TI's place in the formation of the book arises from a heightened awareness that some material in 1–55 seems to have been edited with an eye toward this last section of the book. Thus, in considering this question, scholars have uncovered two possible directions of influence: at some points TI has been influenced by earlier Isaianic material, but at others that earlier material has been edited in the light of TI. Each of these points will be taken up in what follows.

To take the point about allusion first, it is now widely recognized that TI alludes to, and develops, earlier passages from PI and DI. A tidy illustration of this point comes in 57.14-21, a passage which draws on both chs. 6 and 40, to make the point that the old promises retained their validity, but were now limited to the righteous. That the promises were now limited to the righteous is made clear by v. 21, which qualifies the salvation announced in vv. 14-20 with the statement "there is no peace for the wicked." That those promises were drawn from ch. 40 (and were therefore "old") emerges from a comparison of the two passages. The borrowing is clearest in the following verses.

> Comfort, Comfort *my people*, says your God . . . A voice *calling out*: 'In the wilderness *clear the way* of the Lord; In the steppe make straight a *highway* for our God; Let every ravine be *lifted up*; and let every mountain and hill be made low.' (40.1, 3-4)

> *And one says*: '*Cast up, Cast up*; *Clear the way*; *Lift up* the stumbling block from the way of my people.' (57.14)

Several features of the borrowing deserve comment. The latter's command to "cast up" (*slw*) plays on the root consonants of "highway" (*mslh*) in the former. The unidentified voice in 57.14 ("and one says") clearly draws on those voices from 40.3, 6 which appear equally anonymous. In drawing on the earlier passage, ch. 57 transforms it. Where in 40.3 it is the "way of the Lord" that needs to be cleared, in 57.14 it is "the way of my people" that needs this. Moreover, the latter passage adds that it is specifically a "stumbling block" that needs to be cleared, a word absent from the former. Thus, while the "comfort" on offer in ch. 40 remains available in ch. 57 (so v. 18), there is now an obstacle to the people's enjoyment of it. And if v. 21 is any indication, that obstacle was some form of iniquity.

Beyond these points of contact, the borrowing of ch. 40 likely continued on into 58.1-2, the passage immediately following 57.21. Isaiah 58.1-2 looks as though it could be taking up 40.6-9. In both, the commands issue forth to "call out" (40.6; 58.1) and to "lift up your voice" (40.9; 58.1), though the content to be proclaimed differs considerably in each passage, suggesting again that the later text has developed the earlier.

There is a fair measure of agreement that 57.14-21 has taken these allusions to ch. 40 and blended them with subtle references to ch. 6 (likely under the influence of ch. 40's own allusions to this chapter). Thus, when

57.15 calls God the "high and lofty one" (*rm wnś'*), this is almost certainly a reference to 6.1, where, in a vision of the holy one of Israel, Isaiah describes the Lord's throne as "high and lifted up" (*rm wnś'*). The expression *rm wnś'* occurs nowhere else in the Hebrew Bible. Indeed, that this divine title may be a reference to the vision of ch. 6 tends to be strengthened by what follows it in 57.15: "his name is holy." This assertion may well echo the trisagion of 6.2: "holy, holy, holy is the Lord of hosts." And finally, some have found a reversal of 6.10 in 57.18. In the former verse God sends a message to prevent the people from being "healed" (*rp'*), whereas in the latter he promises to "heal" (*rp'*) them. Thus, 57.14-21 blends the allusion to ch. 40 with references to ch. 6.

There are many other instances that could be noted where TI has cited earlier passages in 1–55 (e.g. 11.6-9 in 65.25; 55.5 in 60.9), but the point seems clear enough.

Since TI clearly alludes to passages in 1–55, scholars are now asking whether or not the author/editor of these last 11 chapters of the book may have edited that earlier material. It is usually recognized that he did so by adding 56–66 to that earlier collection. But did he intervene more directly in these chapters? Did he edit them in any way, whether by rearranging pre-existing material, or by adding his own fresh composition? While Elliger (1933) argued that the prophet responsible for TI also arranged the oracles in DI, adding his own composition in the last two chapters, this was not widely accepted, because it depended on the view that the bulk of 56–66 stem from a single individual — a view that has been seriously challenged. That does not mean of course that all of Elliger's examples of redaction are thereby rendered improbable. Since his work, there has been a growing appreciation of the possibility that certain passages in 1–55 have been edited, or composed, in light of TI, so that now one can find monograph-length treatments on the subject.

One treatment deserving special mention is that of Steck (1991), some of his proposals having been influential in subsequent work on this topic (e.g. Berges 1998). Steck argued that TI developed sequentially in four stages, the last three of which were accompanied by book-wide redactions. Each of these book-wide redactions consisted of a layer of additions throughout the book bringing the whole together. The first stage in TI's development came in the mid-fifth century when 60.1–62.7 was written as a literary continuation of an earlier form of 40–55. At that point, DI still circulated independently from an early form of 1–39. The second stage of development saw the joining of this early form of 1–39 with 40–55. This joining also saw the composition of 62.10-12 as a new literary continuation of the whole, as well as the addition of several corresponding texts throughout the book (e.g. 11.11-16). This stage thus involved the creation of a new three-part book of Isaiah (Steck calls it the *Großjesajabuch*). The third stage of TI's development entailed the composition of 56.9–59.21, 63.1-6, and still further additions throughout the book — all of which were to serve a role in uniting the growing corpus. Finally, the fourth stage brought the book into its present form with the addition of a final layer involving 56.1-8, 63.7–66.24, and a fresh set of book-wide additions — again, all of which were composed for their position in the book.

In order, Steck labeled the last three stages of the book's development the "home coming redaction," the "penultimate redaction," and the "final redaction." Each of these he assigned to the Hellenistic period. In sum, Steck argued that each new layer in TI was composed in light of existing Isaianic material, and was part of a redactional layer spanning that corpus.

While my own study seeks to take Steck's findings very seriously, it differs in some important ways from his treatment (Stromberg 2010: 1–7). First, while Steck seeks to identify each reconstructed stage in the growth of TI with a corresponding set of additions and developments within the larger Isaianic corpus, my aim is to examine the role of TI *in its final form* in relation to the formation of the book. As a result, my study uncovers only one layer of redaction in the book that is related to TI. Secondly, several scholars would disagree with Steck when he assigns all of 56.9–59.21 to a layer earlier than 56.1-8 and 65–66. I share their assessment. In an approach like Steck's, a faulty analysis of TI at the outset will lead to skewed conclusions regarding the development of the whole book. The third difference sits at the heart of my study; and that is a comparison of allusion in TI with redaction elsewhere in the book.

To elaborate on this, I would summarize the logic of my study in the following way. After an analysis of the formation of TI, I conclude that the hand responsible for its final form — "the author of TI" — composed 56.1-8 and 65–66, along with other texts. These passages are examined for allusions to earlier Isaianic texts, which helps establish a profile for the author of TI as a reader of the book. This profile is then used as a criterion for identifying instances where he may have acted as a redactor, the argument being that a clear picture of him as reader of the book should provide some insight into how he might have redacted it. This argument has as its premise that his behavior as a redactor will inevitably reflect his behavior as a reader — redactors being readers, and expecting their work to be read. In other words, if some passages in Isaiah were redacted in light of TI (as many claim), then it seems eminently sensible to hold them up to the light of allusion in TI, a light revealing how its author read the book in whatever form it had at the time. In my study, this method illuminates several passages throughout 1–55 that have long been regarded as redactional additions. I argue that these additions were made by the author of TI. Since my own study has yet to be released for publication (at the time I write this), it remains to be seen whether any of its main proposals persuade.

Regardless of the approach taken, there are certain examples of redaction in 1–55 that have long been recognized as related to TI. Perhaps the most widely recognized of these comes in the first chapter of the book at vv. 27-31. This passage shares strong textual parallels with TI, especially with its last two chapters. Both speak of the Lord's saving the repentant (*šwb*) in Zion (1.27; 59.20); both condemn illicit cults related to "tere-binths" (1.29; 57.5) and "gardens" (1.29-30; 65.3; 66.17); in both, the people "choose" (*bḥr*) these things (1.29; 65.12; 66.4); in both, they are described as "the forsakers of the Lord" (1.28; 65.11); in both, they will feel "shame" (*bwš*) for these activities (1.29; 65.13; 66.5); and in both their punishment will be a fire not "quenched" (*kbh*) (1.31; 66.24). The parallels are indeed impressive.

While it is certainly possible to explain these parallels as instances where TI is alluding to an earlier Isaianic text, the evidence overwhelmingly supports viewing these links the other way around. It is more probable that 1.27-31 was written in light of TI. Hence, while it is widely held that ch. 1 brings together genuine material from the ministry of the prophet Isaiah, it is also widely held that the chapter did not receive the form it now has until very much later (for many not until the exilic or post-exilic period). Moreover, five of the shared phrases just noted occur nowhere within the preaching of the prophet Isaiah, either at all or with the particular sense given them in 1.27-31. And this is true even if everything else in 1–39 were ascribed to Isaiah. Thus, the evidence is strongly against seeing 1.27-31 as an authentic oracle from the prophet Isaiah. At the same time, three of the shared terms just noted come only in this passage and TI within the Hebrew Bible, indicating that 1.27-31 was written in light of TI.

Reinforcing the impression that 1.27-31 is a late addition made in light of TI is the widely held opinion that this passage comes as a secondary literary extension of the oracle preceding it in 1.21-26. In contrast to 1.27-31, this oracle is usually ascribed to the prophet Isaiah. It has a clear literary structure that may be illustrated as follows.

```
21a "faithful city"
    21b "judgment," "righteousness"
        22 "dross"
            23 Criticism of the leadership
                24a Divine speech formula
            24b Revenge on the leadership
        25 "dross"
    26a-b "judges," "righteousness"
26b "faithful city"
```

Since 1.27-31 falls outside this structure, it looks all the more like a secondary addition. Most of these facts fail to be accounted for when the above parallels are explained as stemming from TI alluding to ch. 1. Thus, 1.27-31 looks like a late piece of redaction made in light of TI.

While many scholars would agree with this conclusion, it raises a second question that has received less attention. Does this late piece of redactional work stem from the author/redactor responsible for TI, or from a later imitator? Either explanation would account for all of the facts noted above. My own answer, developed in my monograph, is that it stems from the author of TI, and not a later imitator familiar with his work. I arrive at this conclusion on the basis of a comparison of allusion in TI to the manner in which 1.27-31 develops the oracle preceding it in 1.21-26. Without going into all of the detail here, the comparison shows that, at three points, 1.27-31 exhibits precisely the same hermeneutic (i.e. manner of handling the text) as that underlying allusion in TI. Both draw their sources into the cultic issues of their own day (the same issues in each case!); both qualify the second-person speeches made to Zion by introducing a distinction between the righteous and the wicked; and both do so by injecting the element of a necessary response on the part of the individual through repentance. In short, both — the redaction in ch. 1 and allusion in TI — share the same technique and outlook in handling their sources. This strongly suggests that Isa. 1.27-31, rather than being the work of a hand later that TI (and therefore able to imitate it), is actually the product of the same author as those last 11 chapters of the book. Isaiah 1.27-31 stems, in all probability, from the author of TI.

If correct, this conclusion carries with it sweeping implications for the formation of the book as a whole. On this view, it emerges that the same author redacted the first chapter of the book, and composed the last — leading to the impression that he was concerned with the shape of the book as a whole. For this reason, it is only natural to anticipate that he will have played a similar editorial role in the intervening material.

Irrespective of the validity of my own view on this, many scholars regard 1.27-31 as a late piece of redaction made in light of TI. Examples of such redaction can be found in DI as well. We could compare, for example, 48.22 with 57.21, both of which have the same sentence varying only in divine title ("there is no peace for the wicked, says the Lord/my God"). In 48.22, this sentence is widely regarded as secondary, since nothing preceding it really anticipates its thought. By contrast, this sentence is well integrated in 57.21, where it summarizes the thought of vv. 19-20. From these observations, the conclusion quickly emerges that 48.22 was added into that chapter in light of 57.21.

All of this is to illustrate that a lively discussion is now taking place over the role of TI in the formation of the book. And as these examples illustrate, that role entailed not only allusion, but also redaction.

4. Conclusion

The last two chapters have shown that DI and TI both have their own respective shapes and editorial histories, and that the formation of PI can no longer be considered without reference to these later sections of the book. I noted in the conclusion to Chapter 1 that several late additions had been made to PI that focused on exile and restoration. The result of this is that the message of Isaiah the prophet is now seen through the lens of these two pivotal moments in Israel's history. Such a conclusion takes on even greater force, in light of our discussion of chs. 40–66: these final chapters, focusing largely on exile and restoration, have been fully integrated into the book through allusion looking back and redaction looking forward. In this way, PI, and with it the message of Isaiah the prophet, is drawn even deeper into that tragic event of exile and the hope of restoration that sprung from it, both of which exerted tremendous gravity on ancient Israel's thought in the Old Testament. What do the above arguments about the formation of Isaiah suggest for how the book was to be read? That will be discussed in the next two chapters in connection with the idea of a "literary approach."

Chapter 4

Literary Approaches to Isaiah

1. Introduction

A s we turn now to "literary approaches" to Isaiah, the first order of business is that of definition. What is meant by "literary approach"? To get at this we need to consider a phrase sometimes used as a synonym for this, "literary criticism." In biblical studies, this phrase has been employed in two different senses, each of which reflects a separate method of inquiry with its own history. The first use of "literary criticism" refers to the source-oriented analysis of traditional biblical scholarship. This has been accurately described as an "excavative" mode of inquiry as in archeology. Hence, just as archeology seeks to uncover the different periods of occupation at a site by digging down through, and identifying, its various layers, so source-oriented analysis seeks to recover the earlier layers lying behind the final form of a text by identifying, and then peeling away, its later redactions. Ideally (if only so), source-oriented analysis uncovers the earliest textual sources and all subsequent stages of development leading up to the final form of the book. In this sense of the phrase, "literary criticism" has been with us through most of the previous chapters of this book; but that is not the sense with which this chapter is concerned.

The second use of this term stems from outside biblical studies. In a comparatively recent development, biblical scholars have been influenced by a different sort of "literary criticism." Since at least the 1970s, biblical scholarship has come under the influence of the methods developed in the study of comparatively modern literature, such as the English or Russian novel. Hence, it is not at all uncommon to find articles, or even whole books, written on the Bible by professors who hold positions in departments of English literature; it is also not uncommon to find biblical scholars appealing to such studies in their own work. Through a dialogue of scholarship, a whole new line of approach to the Bible has opened up, occasionally replacing (though instead usually supplementing) the older modes of analysis.

But what is "literary criticism" in this sense? What constitutes a "literary approach"? Faced with this question, anyone at all familiar with the study of modern literature will quickly respond that there is no single method, but many; and there are many different (and conflicting) approaches. Indeed, one such scholar, Meir Sternberg who is a professor of poetics and comparative literature, says, "the very phrase 'literary approach' is rather meaningless in view of the diversity of the languages of criticism throughout history, and '*the* literary approach,' with its monolithic ring, is downright misleading" (1985: 3). Sternberg sets out his own very lucid definition of the subject, wherein he identifies discourse-oriented analysis as the root of such study, particularly as this is defined over against the source-oriented analysis of traditional biblical scholarship. In contrast to source-oriented analysis,

> Discourse-oriented analysis . . . sets out to understand not the realities behind the text but the text itself as a pattern of meaning and effect. What does this piece of language — metaphor, epigram, dialogue, tale, cycle, book — signify in context? What are the rules governing the transaction between storyteller or poet and reader? Are the operative rules, for instance, those of prose or verse, parable or chronicle, omniscience or realistic limitation, historical or fictional writing? What image of a world does the narrative project? Why does it unfold the action in this particular order and from this particular viewpoint? What is the part played by the omissions, redundancies, ambiguities, alternations between scene and summary or elevated and colloquial language? How does the work hang together? And, in general, in what relationship does the part stand to whole and form to function? (Sternberg 1985: 15).

Thus, a literary approach has at its core an interest in *what* a literary text means, and *how* it means it. And as Sternberg has framed it, "this line of questioning is to make sense of the discourse in terms of communication, always goal-directed on the speaker's part and always requiring interpretive activity on the addressee's" (1985: 15). To seek the meaning of a literary text is to become an active recipient of an act of communication with rules that govern the transaction.

While a "literary approach," being grounded in discourse-oriented analysis, differs in its aim from source-oriented interests, the two are nevertheless closely related. In as far as a literary analysis of Isaiah seeks to enable a better reading of it, this approach is an indispensable component of the other avenues of inquiry into the text. Using Isaiah as a record for recovering "what happened," probing its depths to uncover the sources incorporated into it, or seeking to discern its theological voice — all these endeavors entail reading the text. And deeper insight into how the text was to be read can be gained by attention to the literary conventions governing it. These conventions are the concern of a literary approach. Thus, literary criticism offers greater precision to these other endeavors, since these endeavors all assume a reading of the text — even if that itself is not their final destination.

To illustrate the point, if one wishes to uncover the sources underlying the present form of the book of Isaiah, one must infer them through a careful reading of the book *as we have it*, the present form of the book being for the most part our only evidence (excepting of course 2 Kgs 18.13–20.19 from which Isaiah 36–39 was taken). Thus, competent reading of the text must precede competent excavation of the source. "[H]ypotheses about source stand or fall on the cogency of the analysis of discourse" (Sternberg 1985: 17). Indeed, for many, this new awareness of the Bible's complex workings as literature has called into question many of the tell-tale signs of source and redaction observed by the older source-oriented approach of biblical scholarship. In many cases, a rough edge in the text previously explained by appeal to textual pre-history is now seen to contribute to purposive composition, making the older appeal to source unnecessary. Many biblical stories, for example, which were once thought to be a jumble of sources are now being explained as meaningful wholes, whose artful design serves specific communicative ends. In this way, literary artistry has rightly taken its place alongside mechanical compilation as a possible explanation of the shape of biblical texts, Isaiah included.

At the same time, Sternberg and many others advocating a "literary approach" would scarcely deny that many stories, passages, and books of the Bible are of a composite nature (e.g. Alter 1981: 19–20). In these cases, competent reading is informed by competent excavation. Awareness of the composite nature of a book like Isaiah enables the reader to begin to judge which features of the text are attributable to source, and which to strategy. The judgment will, of course, depend on the pre-disposition of the individual reader, that being informed not least by the theory of composition that is held. While the judgment will therefore be subjective, it is unavoidable, at least for anyone wishing to engage the vast ocean of scholarship that surrounds Isaiah. It is unavoidable for the simple reason that Isaiah incorporates both source and literary strategy, so that the reader who wishes to make sense of it must maintain a balance between these two frames of reference; and this whether he wishes to uncover an earlier layer or discern purposive discourse. In Isaiah, he will be confronted with both.

From these few brief comments, it should be clear that a "literary approach" — in as far as it seeks to enable competent reading — is indispensable to the other avenues of inquiry surveyed in this book.

To clarify what this approach entails, we should consider a common conception of the literary study of the Bible, one that underlies the notion of studying "the Bible *as* literature." To the extent that this reflects an attempt to study it "as" literature even if in some sense it is "not," it entails an unfortunate "divorce between method and object" (Sternberg 1985: 4). However, since many would judge the Bible (Isaiah included) to be a literary text, they see a literary approach as justified: literary text, literary approach.

Besides this, the phrase has implied another unhappy separation. More than once, scholars have studied the literary features of the Bible *in isolation* from its communicative aims, from its theological or ideological point. This could be thought of as a purely aesthetic appreciation of the text. But in Isaiah (as in the rest of the Bible) literary features are a means to an end; they are the building blocks of a rhetoric that seeks to persuade. There is very little art for art's sake. Thus, this approach rends the biblical aesthetic — its artful forms of discourse — out of its native context, the communicative aims of the text, be they theological or other. As Fishbane (1981: 100) puts it, "What the text has joined together let no critic rend asunder: form and content constitute an indissoluble whole." Or, as Alter (1981: 19) states, "Rather than viewing the literary character of the Bible as one of several 'purposes' or 'tendencies' . . ., I would prefer to insist on a complete interfusion of literary art with theological, moral, or historiosophical vision, the fullest perception of the latter dependent on the fullest grasp of the former."

Finally, a third separation, sometimes implicit in efforts to study "the Bible as literature" arises from the move to pit a literary interest in the text against a historical one. In as far as this seeks to articulate the distinction between source- and discourse-oriented analyses noted above, the move has merit. But if it aims to study the Bible in isolation from the history out of which it arose and to which it addresses itself, then it fails as soon as the barrier of language is encountered. For the Bible is written in Classical Hebrew, the language of the ancient Israelites, and this is no less a historical datum than any other — the language infusing, and being infused with, the culture of that time. Thus, just as the Bible is not literature as opposed to theology (but for the sake of it), so it is not literature as opposed to history (but grounded in it). A literary approach to Isaiah which strives for the happy union of object and method will resist separating these aspects of the text, seeking instead to view them in their proper inter-relation.

As an approach grounded in the study of discourse, literary criticism has introduced into biblical studies a keen awareness of the role of the reader. In a very real sense, texts only *mean* when an audience reads (or listens to) them. For some scholars, this realization has erased the validity of seeking what it was that the author of the text was trying to communicate. Here, the dominant metaphor is that readers — whether ancient or modern — "construct" a text's meaning. However, as the discussion of Sternberg above indicates, an awareness of the role of the reader need not lead to this one-sided conclusion. Since authors produce texts to communicate something or achieve some effect, we could speak of the reading process as "accessing" or "activating" a text's meaning, rather than as "constructing" it. To readers familiar with the "Intentional Fallacy" debate, I would recommend Sternberg's discussion of "external" versus "embodied intention" (1985: 8–9). His approach reasonably focuses on "embodied intention," wherein "'intention' no longer figures as a psychological state consciously on unconsciously translated into words. Rather, it is a shorthand for the structure of meaning and effect supported by the conventions that the text appeals to or devises; for the sense that language makes in terms of the communicative context as a whole." Hence, we need not dispense with the author's intention when seeking to understand the text. Nevertheless, literary theory has heightened our awareness of the active role readers play in enabling texts to mean — a point duly noted by scholars of Isaiah (e.g. Conrad 1991, Darr 1994).

In the light of all that a literary approach might mean for the Bible in general, we may ask: what has it meant for Isaiah in particular? Proposals on Isaiah differ, just as methods in the field of literary criticism differ. However, if there is one common theme that surfaces time and again in literary treatments of Isaiah, it is the desire to offer a holistic reading. This desire flows naturally from a literary approach, since such an approach has at its core the discourse-oriented task of seeking meaningful coherence in a text's final form (for exceptions, see Gunn 2000). Literary readings with this holistic focus have been offered for the book as a whole (Webb 1990), as well as for sub-collections within it (Exum 1979). While these approaches share the conviction that a meaningful holistic reading is possible, they do not necessarily operate on the assumption that the passage examined was written from the very beginning by a single author. The passage could just as well be the result of an editor's effort to combine disparate sources. For example, Exum, who adopts "a literary perspective," agrees with most scholars "that Is 28-32 is a collection . . . of independent oracles from different situations." But, she seeks nevertheless "to study the effect produced when the material . . . is read as a literary whole" — this effort arising out of an interest "in the meaning the prophetic words take on in light of their present context" (1979: 123). Such literary readings of Isaiah, as we shall later see, are developed in various ways: some scholars, for example, appeal to the role of readers in "constructing" meaning, while others look to the role of redactors in constructing texts.

Whatever else a literary approach entails, it will most certainly interest itself in the literary features of Isaiah and their meaningful employment in the book. This chapter will examine some of these features, and the next will probe more closely the literary notion of a holistic reading of Isaiah.

2. Literary Features of Isaiah

a. Poetry

When it comes to the Hebrew Bible, the line between poetry and prose is not always an easy one to draw. But, by any account, Isaiah is full of poetry. Indeed, poetry appears regularly in the prophetic books in general, suggesting the prophets, whose words are preserved in these books, employed this artful form of discourse in their ministries. As Alter notes, their work involved delivering prophetic discourse, a discourse which "in the vast majority of instances . . . is not, in formal terms, the prophet who is speaking but God Who is speaking through the prophet's quotation" (1985: 140). Thus, the prophetic poetry of Isaiah is frequently punctuated with phrases like "thus says the Lord." As to why poetry was felt to be an especially appropriate form for the divine discourses delivered by the prophets, Alter poses the following question: "If we could actually hear God talking, making His will manifest in words of the Hebrew language, what would He sound like?" The answer, he proposes, is the following:

> Since poetry is our best human model of intricately rich communication, not only solemn, weighty, and forceful but also densely woven with complex internal connections, meanings, and implications, it makes sense that divine speech should be represented as poetry (1985: 141).

If such was the convention in ancient Israel, then the very choice to use poetry as a means of discourse says something about the content of that discourse — in this case, that it presents itself as divine. Hence, if Alter is correct, literary form and meaning are inseparable in the poetry of Isaiah.

Whether for this reason or for some other, the book of Isaiah speaks primarily in poetry, so that a few words about its workings are in order here. The poetry of Isaiah is of course unique to the book in some respects, but it also shares the characteristics of biblical poetry more broadly, a subject which has attracted a good deal of attention (Kugel 1981). Of the many features of this poetry, some are evident only in Hebrew. Take, for example, the play on sound in the following two passages, whose Hebrew transliteration is modified from Schöckel (1987: 182).

> *boqeq ... bolqah ... hiboq tiboq ha'arets*
> *hiboz tiboz ...*
> *'abela nabela ha'arets*
> *'umlalah nabelah tebel.* (Isa. 24.1-4)

> *ro'ah hitro'e'ah ha'arets*
> *por hitporerah 'erets*
> *mot hitmotetah 'arets*
> *no'a tanu'a 'erets.* (Isa. 24.19-20)

These two passages describe the violent shaking of the earth in divine judgment, both playing with sound in a way that Schöckel describes as "an onomatopoetic parade" roughly equivalent to the English "the earth shivers and staggers, stumbles and tumbles, quivers and quavers and quakes, jars and jerks and jolts." The prophet weaves the event's disturbing motion directly into the aural fabric of the poem, meaning permeating form. In no uncertain terms, the rhetorical shape of the passage warns the readers of universal judgment.

Sound play is only one among many techniques employed in biblical poetry, and by no means is it the most pervasive one (Watson 1994). The most pervasive feature of this form of discourse is probably parallelism (Berlin 1992). Fortunately, parallelism, unlike sound play, frequently comes across in translation, even if only imperfectly. Berlin defines parallelism "as the repetition of the same or related semantic content and/or grammatical structure in consecutive lines or verses" (1992: 155). For example, in Ps. 103.10, the first line matches the second in both sense and structure.

> Not according to our sins did he deal with us;
> and not according to our transgressions did he repay us.

Berlin gives a helpful taxonomy of the ways in which parallelism works itself out at all levels of language in biblical poetry. Using her categories, we may list a few examples of parallelism from Isaiah's poetry here.

(1) *The Grammatical Aspect:* "In grammatical parallelism the syntax of the lines is equivalent" (1992: 158). While Berlin has in mind a more complex notion of syntax than merely the surface structure of a sentence, the latter is apparent in Isa. 40.18.

> To whom can you liken God?
> And what likeness can you compare to him?

In this case, each line begins with an interrogative of identity ("to whom"/"what likeness"). In each line, this is then followed by a second person masculine plural verb of comparison ("can you liken"/"can you compare"). Both lines then conclude with a reference to God ("God"/"to him").

(2) *The Lexical Aspect:* This form of parallelism entails "the pairing of associated words," which can occur in lines that are not grammatically parallel (1992: 159). Consider Isa. 54.2:

> Enlarge the place of your tent;
> and let the curtains of your dwellings be extended . . .

In this example, "tent" parallels "curtains" of "dwellings." The pairing of words in such parallelism can appear in a variety of forms.

(3) *The Semantic Aspect:* This aspect "pertains to the relationship between the meaning of the parallel lines" (1992: 159). Like word pairings, the semantic aspect encompasses several different relations between the paralleled elements.

> Ascend a high hill, herald (to) Zion;
> Lift your voice aloud, herald (to) Jerusalem. (Isa. 40.9)

In this example from the first chapter of DI, the semantic relationship between the lines is complex. On the one hand, there is development between the two lines: the herald's actions are sequential, first ascending a hill, then lifting up the voice. On the other hand, the second line restates the first, substituting "Jerusalem" for "Zion." Thus, the line exhibits both aspects of semantic parallelism discussed by Berlin, who employs linguistic categories in her analysis. The development reflects a syntagmatic response, which involves "the choice of an associate from the same sequence rather than the same class." The restatement displays a paradigmatic operation, wherein "a word is chosen from the same category and may substitute for the given word" (1992: 159).

(4) *The Phonological Aspect:* This entails sound equivalences which "may be activated in parallelism just as grammatical and lexical equivalences are" (1992: 159). This often takes the form of sound pairs as in Isa. 40.12a.

Who measured in the hollow of his hand the waters (*mym*);
and the sky (*šmym*) with a span meted out?

Berlin's analysis of parallelism, more sophisticated than these few examples would suggest, is only one among many such studies. But as these
examples show, this feature of biblical poetry is well represented in the
book of Isaiah; and renewed appreciation of this feature is one of the many
fruits now being born by literary interests in the Hebrew Bible.

Like parallelism, metaphor is not limited to poetry. But it does occur in
poetry with great frequency — especially in the poetry of Isaiah. Several
studies of metaphor in Isaiah have now appeared, drawing attention to
its central role in various levels of the book's composition (e.g. Moughtin-
Mumby 2008, Nielsen 1989). As is evident from a comparison of these
works, there are different theories about metaphor and therefore different
categories used in metaphor analysis. Perhaps it is sufficient here simply
to note one central metaphor used throughout the book of Isaiah, one
bound up with its central theme.

Zion's destiny is arguably the most pervasive theme in the book, and
a key metaphor depicting it is "Zion as woman." In the book, this metaphor appears in a variety of forms: e.g. Zion as prostitute, as mother, as
barren woman, as God's wife. Such variety is no doubt due in part to the
fact that the book is the product of many different hands; and it urges
the careful reader to discern the unique shape of each example without
necessarily trying blend them all together into a single picture. This point
can be illustrated through a few examples.

In the very first chapter of the book, Zion, the once "faithful city," is
said to have turned into a "prostitute" (1.21). In the metaphor, the city
itself is said to be a woman, and what her turning into a prostitute means
is clarified in vv. 21b-23. The city, once full of "justice" and "righteousness," is now full of "murderers." Central to her sad transformation
was a corrupt leadership, one that "loves bribes and pursues gifts," but
does not attend to the needs of the "orphan" and "widow." That it was
her leadership that defiled her is further elaborated in vv. 24-26. In these
verses, God promises Zion that he will remove her corrupt leadership,
replacing it with the judges and counselors she once had — thereby
restoring her former noble status: "Afterwards you will be called City of
Righteousness, Faithful City" (v. 26). She will be known once again by
her former name (cf. 62.2 where an identical construction clearly indicates
the issue of status). Given that vv. 21-26 place the fault squarely on the
leadership while saying nothing about Zion's own choice in the matter,
the metaphor describing her transformation into a prostitute paints her
more as the victim than perpetrator of the crime, though the loss of her
former status as "faithful" does seem to implicate her as well. In any case,
vv. 21-26 never explicitly depict Zion as a wife or as a mother, but only
as a woman whose status has been tarnished and needs to be restored.

The metaphor of "Zion as woman" surfaces in a very different way
in 37.22, the first verse of the "word which the Lord spoke" concerning
the impending Assyrian siege of Jerusalem. In this poem, God promises

to repel the threat, sending the Assyrians back along the road upon which they came (v. 29). The "word" from the Lord addresses the Assyrian king directly, and shows him blatant scorn by depicting Zion as a young woman mocking him. "The virgin, daughter Zion, despises you, she mocks you; daughter Jerusalem shakes her head behind you" (v. 22). The prophetic poem bolsters confidence in the coming deliverance through defiant metaphor. So certain is that deliverance that the threatened city is personified as a woman who shows no fear of (and even despises) the aggressor, an aggressor far superior in military might. This is of course a very different use of the metaphor of "Zion as woman" than was encountered in Isa. 1.21, which called Jerusalem a "prostitute" in need of redemption from within.

The "virgin" Zion who mocks her enemies out of overwhelming confidence in divine deliverance is a metaphor differing also from that found in Isa. 49.14-23, where Zion is a mother bereaved of her children. With the Babylonian destruction of Jerusalem came the exile of its population, here pictured as children of her bereavement. Zion complains "the Lord has forsaken me; and God has forgotten me" (v. 14). In a comforting tone typical of DI, God responds in a brief reversal of metaphor, assuring her that his commitment is like that of a woman to her newborn child. Taking up her complaint, he asks "Will a woman forget her suckling child, the compassionate one, the child of her womb?" Then, trumping the force of the metaphor itself, he says that "even if these should forget, I will not forget you" (v. 15). Thus, shifting back to Zion as woman, he tells her to lift up her eyes and see that he is bringing her children back. "The children of your bereavement will again say in your hearing, 'this place is too small for us . . .'" (v. 20). Zion, formerly childless, will have more children than she has space. She will say to herself in utter amazement, "who gave birth to these?" and "I was bereaved and barren . . . who raised these up?" (v. 21). The metaphor comes to full force in v. 22 with a divine promise to the childless woman:

> Behold I will lift up my hand to the nations;
> and to the peoples I will raise my signal;
> then they will bring your sons on the bosom;
> and your daughters on the shoulder will be carried.

Here the metaphor describing Zion is far from that of the confident virgin in 37.22, or the faithless prostitute in 1.21. Here she is a woman, alone (v. 21) and bereaved, a woman whose grief has fallen on the ears of a God eager to restore those she had lost.

It is clear from these few examples, to which more could easily be added, that the metaphor of "Zion as woman" appears in a variety of forms in the book, each form being uniquely suited to the rhetorical situation to which the poem was originally addressed — the first to a pre-exilic city loaded with sin, the second to a pre-exilic city faced with annihilation by an invading army, and the third to a city sitting alone with its population in exile.

While each of these metaphors has its own unique shape, there is evidence in the book itself that they were being combined in the latest layers of Isaiah, giving birth to new composite images whose metaphorical force depended as much on being conscious allusion to the earlier passages as it did on its own originality.

One striking example of this late blending of Isaianic metaphor comes in the poetry of Isa. 66.7-14 which imagines Zion as a mother of a righteous sub-group within the people, a group called God's "servants."

To build its case that these pious few would be the true heirs of the earlier Isaianic promises, this passage draws together several elements from the "Zion as woman" metaphor found throughout the book. To assure this group of their deliverance from persecution (v. 5), the poem begins with a child-bearing metaphor in vv. 7-9, whose logic probably runs as follows: if Zion goes into labor she will have success in giving birth to her children; therefore, your current suffering guarantees your immanent deliverance. That the pious "servants" are identified as Zion's children is confirmed by what follows in vv. 10-14 where the servants are promised they will "suckle" and "be sated from the breast of [Zion's] comforts" (v. 11). Because this group expected its deliverance to come in the form described by earlier Isaianic prophecies whose fulfillment they awaited, the poem in 66.7-14 draws from *and combines* elements of several of these earlier poems promising salvation to Zion and her population. It is probable, for example, that 66.8-9 draws from 37.3 and 54.1, and 66.12 from 49.22 and 60.4 (Stromberg 2010: 109–114).

That the effort was to appropriate the older promises for this particular group is evident in several of the reuses. Hence, where 54.11 identifies mother Zion as the one in need of "comfort," 66.13 develops this by promising her children, "you will be comforted," "you will be sated from the breast of her comforts." And again, where 49.22 promises Zion, "*Your daughters* will be carried on the shoulder," 66.12 transforms this, offering comfort to her persecuted children, "*You* will be carried on the hip." In both instances, the allusion drops the feminine singular addressing Zion in favor of a masculine plural addressing her children. Since her children are identified in this new context with the pious servants (v. 14), this move entailed a clear transfer of the older promises to them. Thus, older poetic metaphors are synthesized in this later passage.

The point here is to illustrate the rich use of metaphor in Isaiah's poetry, and to sensitize the reader both to the particular shape of each image used and to later syntheses of these images in the book. In both cases, we see yet again how Isaianic prophecy employs literary form to its own ideological end.

b. Allusion

It should be clear by now that Isaiah was not written in a cultural vacuum. Rather, like any literary text, it is permeated with the culture it seeks to address. This includes the literary tradition of that culture or surrounding

cultures, which brings us to the next literary feature of Isaiah to be discussed: its artful use of other texts. Part of Isaiah's rhetoric is achieved
by making overt references to other texts that would have been familiar
to its readers/hearers. The reuse of earlier texts by later ones has been the
subject of considerable attention in literary studies and has now made
major inroads into biblical studies (Schultz 1999). This is especially true
of work on Isaiah (e.g. Nurmela 2006, Sommer 1998). Accordingly, our
own discussion has already drawn attention to several instances where the
parts of Isaiah written later allude to the parts written earlier. However,
it remains for us to define more clearly the categories scholars employ
in analyzing these types of textual relations. Since such categories have
received far less attention from biblical scholars than they deserve, we will
devote more time to them here than might otherwise be justified. It also
remains to discuss Isaiah's use of other biblical texts.

A helpful analytical map for the study of this feature of discourse has
been drawn by Sommer in his study of Isaiah 40–66, tellingly titled *A
Prophet Reads Scripture* (1998). To begin, Sommer differentiates "influence" and "allusion" from "intertextuality." According to Sommer, in
scholarly discourse:

> [I]ntertextuality is concerned with the reader or with the text as a thing independ-
> ent of its author, while influence and allusion are concerned with the author as
> well as the text and reader. Intertextuality is synchronic in its approach, influ-
> ence or allusion diachronic or even historicist. Intertextuality is interested in a
> very wide range of correspondences among texts, influence and allusion with a
> more narrow set. Intertextuality examines the relations among many texts, while
> influence and allusion look for specific connections between a limited number
> of texts (1998: 8).

The crucial difference between these two notions is that allusion and
influence ask "how one composition evokes its antecedents, how one
author is affected by another, and what sources a text utilizes" (1998: 6).
In other words, this approach would seek to distinguish between "the
earlier text (the source or the influence) and the later one (the alluding
text or the influenced)." The approach is therefore diachronic, seeking
to understand the relationship between earlier and later texts "through
time." For various reasons that can not be dealt with here, intertextuality
does not necessarily concern itself with establishing which text was first
and which last, or which text influenced the other (1998: 7). A recent study
of Isaiah 24–27 from this perspective is that of Polaski (2001); also see the
nuanced discussion of this by Hays (2008) and compare Miscall (1992).
At this point, Sommer has identified an important distinction between the
two lines of inquiry, his own study settling on the categories of influence
and allusion. Thus, he seeks to identify instances where a later author
consciously refers to an antecedent text in his own writing. Such will be
the approach in the examples that follow.

Sommer's analytical map includes several other important categories.
He distinguishes "allusion" from "influence." In the case of allusion, the

author refers in his or her own writing to another text, and provides a textual marker intended to enable a reader to recognize that reference. In such an instance, some aspect of the meaning or effect of the new text will depend on the reader's ability to recognize the reference and interpret its significance. To interpret the reference the reader is expected to "bring certain elements of the evoked text . . . to bear on the alluding text, and these alter the reader's construal of the meaning of the sign in the alluding text" (1998: 12). At times, to achieve the desired effect, the reader is expected to activate "the evoked text as a whole to form connections between it and the alluding text," connections not explicitly given in the alluding text (1998: 12). In other words, texts laden with allusion require readers to recognize the references and interpret their effect. Otherwise some aspect of the text's pattern of meaning will be lost. By contrast, influence, rather than dealing with "the *use* to which the earlier text is put in the new one," examines a much broader phenomenon than allusion: "influence refers to relations between authors, whole works, and even traditions" (Sommer 1998: 14–15). This has less to do with *how* texts mean.

Also to be distinguished from "allusion" is the category of "exegesis" by which Sommer means "an attempt to analyze, explain, or give meaning to (or uncover meaning in) a text." The two are different in function, though they can overlap. As he puts it, "An exegetical text clarifies or transforms an earlier text; an allusive text utilizes a earlier text" (1998: 18). Allusions "utilize" their sources for any number of reasons — "to bolster the authority of the work," to "bolster the authority of a predecessor's work," "to distance the new work from the old," to "establish a link between author and audience," to "allow the author to display his or her erudition," to give "the readers an opportunity to demonstrate their knowledge," to give pleasure "to authors and readers alike," "to introduce less well-known works into a canon or to create a new canon" (Sommer 1998: 18–19). Clearly allusion, though often subtle, is laden with potential, potential to orient readers and position texts within societies.

In large part, Sommer's methodological discussion leaves unaddressed the question of how modern scholars are to go about identifying probable instances of such textual relations, a problematic task since the recognition of these relations was closely bound to a culture that is now removed from our own by over 2,000 years. He certainly recognizes the problem, and argues accordingly in many of his textual analyses later in the book. However, it would be helpful here to list some criteria for establishing the probability of allusion, influence, and the like. Here Christopher Hays (2008: 36–41) has given a helpful list of criteria derived from Richard Hays' work on "echoes" of the Old Testament in the New (2005: 25–49). These criteria may simply be listed in the form given.

1. Availability: Was the proposed source of the echo available to the author and/ or his original readers? 2. Volume: How "loud" is the echo; that is, how explicit and overt is it? 3. Recurrence or Clustering: How often does the author cite or allude to the same text? 4. Thematic Coherence: How well does the alleged

echo fit into the line of argument of the passage in question? Does the proposed precursor text fit together with the point the author is making? 5. Historical Plausibility: Could an author in fact have intended the alleged meaning effect of any proposed allusion, and could contemporaneous readers have understood it? 6. History of Interpretation: Have other readers in the tradition heard the same echoes that we now think we hear? 7. Satisfaction: Does the proposed intertextual reading illuminate the surrounding discourse and make some larger sense of the author's argument as a whole? Do we find ourselves saying, "Oh, so *that's* what the author meant"?

These guides would serve admirably in analyzing "echo" in the Hebrew Bible, though Christopher Hays rightly places a caveat on the fourth point, noting that biblical authors can also *subvert* their sources, generating a sense of discontinuity — a point that comports well with Sommer's observation that allusion can serve "to distance the new work from the old."

These are a few of the categories scholars have developed in analyzing various forms of textual dependence (a more developed approach can be found in Lyons 2009: 47–75). Since there is a danger that this whole discussion may seem abstract and perhaps condensed (though necessarily so), we would do well to illustrate the issues at stake with a few examples of this literary feature in Isaiah. In order, we will look at Isaiah's use of Isaiah, and then its use of other biblical texts.

As we have already seen, later Isaianic texts can refer to earlier Isaianic texts. Thus, we have given many examples of how DI and TI take up earlier parts of the book. One further example of this should suffice here. The following example is perhaps the most conspicuous instance of inner-Isaianic referencing in the whole book, and thus offers a solid case for illustrating method.

Isaiah 65.25 has long been regarded as a condensed citation of 11.6-9. The latter reads,

> And the *wolf* will dwell with the *lamb*,
>> the leopard will lie down with the young goat,
> the calf and the lion and the fatling together,
>> and a young child will lead them;
> The cow and bear will *graze together*,
>> their children will lie down;
>> *and a lion will eat straw like an ox.*
> An infant will play over the hole of the *asp*,
>> and over the den of the *viper* a weaned child will stretch his hand.
> *They will neither harm nor destroy on all my holy mountain*, because the land
>> will be full of the knowledge of the Lord as the waters cover the sea.

In a clear parallel to this passage, Isa. 65.25 promises,

> *Wolf* and *lamb will graze together and a lion will eat straw like an ox*, but a *snake* shall eat dust; *they will neither harm nor destroy on all my holy mountain*, says the Lord.

That there is a direct literary relationship between these two passages seems beyond dispute (compare the italicized material above). Moreover, that 65.25 should be the later alluding text and 11.6-9 the earlier evoked text is entirely reasonable, given that ch. 65 was written in the post-exilic period and at least part of ch. 11 was probably written in the pre-exilic period. And this view — that 65.25 is literarily dependent on 11.6-9 — is in fact the majority view. However, as Schultz (1999: 240–255) notes, there is room for disagreement. It is not impossible that 11.6-9 is the later of the two, so that instead it refers to 65.25. In all such cases of evaluating literary dependence, probability would seem the best guide. Absolute certainty is a rare gift in biblical studies. Despite disagreement, it would seem that probability favors 65.25 as the later alluding text. One important piece of evidence is the different words for "together" used in each passage. Since we have already established that the two passages are related, these two different expressions for "together" must also be related. We can therefore ask whether this difference sheds any light on the issue. Indeed it does. Whereas 11.6-7 employs a very common expression for "together" (yḥdw), 65.25 uses one that is found only otherwise in very late passages (kʾḥd) — a detail best accounted for on the view that 65.25 is indeed the later of the two passages. It cites the earlier 11.6-9 and updates its diction for a later period (Driver 1920: 240). Several other details support this conclusion (Stromberg 2010: 101–109).

Having determined the direction of influence, we are left with the question of meaning. Why did the author of 65.25 cite 11.6-9? How was the reader to have interpreted this citation? What was its significance? To get at this, the reader has to compare the form of each passage, and consider both contexts, that of the evoked text (11.6-9) and that of the alluding text (65.25).

First of all, it is obvious that the allusion in 65.25 reaffirms the future hope described in 11.6-9, affirming the authority of the earlier vision by giving it new life in the later post-exilic context within which the later was written. Because ch. 65 is post-exilic, its reaffirmation of 11.6-9 projects this earlier vision *beyond the exile*. While this may seem like an unremarkable conclusion in the light of the fact that 11.10-16 paints a picture of restoration after exile, these verses are very widely thought to be a later addition to the chapter, so that in theory the author of ch. 65 could have been reading 11.1-9 before it was combined with these later verses. And it should be carefully noted that nothing in 11.1-9 speaks of exile, let alone restoration from exile. The move to project the vision of 11.6-9 beyond the exile by citing it in 65.25 is therefore noteworthy. Of course, had 11.10-16 been in place when the author of ch. 65 read 11.1-9, the move to project the vision in this way would have been entirely in keeping with the reading context. Indeed, that the author of ch. 65 does make this move may even be seen as support that by the time he read 11.1-9, it was already joined with 11.10-16 into a single vision describing a future king who would signal the end of exile and beginning of national restoration. Isaiah 11.10 joins the two oracles by identifying the king of 11.1 ("the branch from the stock of Jesse") with the "signal" of 11.12

that would be raised to the nations, initiating return and national restoration. Thus, in 11.10 it is "the root of Jesse" who "stands as a signal to the nations."

While 65.25 therefore clearly reaffirms the vision of 11.6-9 projecting it beyond the exile, there remains a less obvious issue in interpreting the allusion, and that is whether or not the allusion was to evoke the content of 11.1-5 — the description of the future Davidic king — which is not formally cited. Why did this later author quote 11.6-9 but not 11.1-5?

According to Sommer, this shows that 65.25 ignores 11.1-9's "references to the king by shifting its predictions regarding the Davidic line to the people as a whole" (1998: 84, 87 nt. 40). However, one may question whether any such shift really takes place in our passage. In both 11.6-9 and 65.25 the people enjoy the peace described, so that there is no transformation of this aspect. But more importantly, in 11.1-9 the king, acting as divine agent, effects the peace through his just reign, a role that is decidedly not transferred to the people in 65.25. There is no indication in ch. 65 that the people (rather than the king) bring about the conditions described there. There, peace is brought by divine action, precisely the same mode underlying the idea of the king as divine agent in 11.1-9. Thus, 65.25 shows itself a rather poor example of the principle Sommer seeks to illustrate.

Moreover, part of the force of Sommer's argument depends on seeing 40–66 as a composition wholly independent from 1–39, a view that was once widely held, but which has become untenable in light of research on the composition of the book (see Chapters 1–3 above). Chapters 40–66 are now seen as having been *written onto* earlier material in 1–39, rather than as having been secondarily *attached to* these earlier chapters at a very late date. This is the case for 40–55 and especially for 56–66. Chapters 40–66, rather than having been conceived of as a different work, were composed from the very beginning as a continuation of 1–39. Indeed, seen in this light, the author of TI will have been the very one responsible for preserving the older oracle in ch. 11, so that it is difficult to see how he would have effectively rejected its central point. By saying that he wrote his own work (56–66) as an extension of the older Isaianic oracles, scholars are in effect saying that he *incorporated* this older material into his work, thereby preserving it for posterity. And it is clear that he sought to preserve the older material — the oracle about the Davidic king in 11.1-9 included — because he deemed it divinely inspired. Thus, when he cites 11.6-9 in 65.25, he adds the phrase "Says the Lord," indicating his high valuation of the older oracles. For this reason, one might reasonably question whether the author of TI, who in this way preserved the oracle in 11.1-9 because he thought it was divinely inspired, would really have rejected the central assertion of that passage. All this is to say that Sommer's argument, to the extent that it is predicated on viewing 40–66 as a separate literary work, needs to be re-evaluated.

An alternative to Sommer's view is suggested by Schultz, who observes that how one understands 65.25 should depend on whether or not it is supposed to evoke "the entire content of 11.1-9" (1999: 256). As Sommer himself notes, allusion requires that readers "bring certain elements of the evoked text . . . to bear on the alluding text, and these alter the reader's construal of the meaning of the sign in the alluding text" (1998: 12). While this description would apply to his analysis of the citation in 65.25, it would equally apply to the possibility suggested by Schultz. It is entirely possible that the reader of 65.25 was to be reminded of the whole content of 11.1-9, the later allusion thereby activating the royal expectations of the earlier oracle for the later reader.

Is there any evidence either in the form or in the content of the passages that such evocation was operative? Two textual details suggest that it was. First, this is suggested by the form of the citation in 65.25. Out of all the inner-Isaianic references in the book, this one stands out as the clearest instance of quotation. With regard to the relationship between the form and function of quotation, Lyons notes that "the quality and quantity of borrowed material are important factors, because these relate to the reader's ability to detect the presence of borrowed material" (2009: 55–56). The reader's ability to detect such borrowed material is important because they "must recognize the link to the source text in order for the quotation to function . . ." (2009: 57). It is this clear link to the source text that one would expect in a case of evocation such as that suggested by Schulz, so that the form of quotation in 65.25 probably indicates that its author sought to draw the reader's attention to the whole vision of ch. 11, rather than to just vv. 6-9 of that vision.

Second, if the form of 65.25 suggests a broader evocation of the whole of 11.1-9, then the content of that earlier oracle would have almost certainly lead such a later reader, for whom it was being evoked, to *re*anticipate the royal promise of 11.1-9. The reason for this is simple. The peaceful vision of 11.6-9 is causally dependent on the reign of the king in 11.1-5. For 11.1-9, without the king there would be no peace. Accordingly, if the form of 65.25 drew the reader back to the vision of 11.1-9, there he would draw the inevitable conclusion that the future peace and therefore the king who would bring it remained firmly on the horizon of the future.

While such a conclusion would certainly not go unchallenged, I regard it as probable. But the point here is to illustrate the importance of inner-Isaianic allusion as a literary feature of the book. A reader who lacks sensitivity to these surface structures of the text will inevitably miss whole worlds of meaning lying underneath them, even if those worlds remain a challenge to uncover.

Passages in Isaiah also allude to other biblical texts. Sticking with our example from 65.25, we may note a subtle allusion to Genesis 3 where the "snake" is cursed to a diet of dust for his role in deceiving Eve.

Comparing 65.25 to its source text in 11.6-9, we note a subtle difference. Where 11.8 states that "an infant will play over the hole of the asp, and over the den of the viper a weaned child will stretch his hand," 65.25 replaces this with "but a snake shall eat dust." That the one substitutes for the other is clear both because of the references to snakes in each of these phrases and because each is preceded and followed by language identical to that found in the other passage (see the bold material below for both of these points).

Isaiah 11.7-9	Isaiah 65.25
and a lion will eat straw like an ox.	and a lion will eat straw like an ox,
An infant will play over the hole of the **asp**, and over the den of the **viper** a weaned child will stretch his hand.	but a **snake** shall eat dust.
They will neither harm nor destroy on all my holy mountain.	They will neither harm nor destroy on all my holy mountain.

Clearly the reference to the "snake" in 65.25 was inspired by the "asp" and "viper" of 11.8. But why did the alluding author change the word? Moreover, it is evident from the context in 11.6-9 that the point in mentioning the animals is that the dangerous ones will no longer pose a threat to the vulnerable ones: "a lion will eat straw like an ox." Each will cohabit with the other in peace: wolf with lamb, leopard with young goat, lion with calf, bear with cow, and, in the audacious assertion of 11.8, infant with asp and viper. As 11.9 puts it, "they will neither harm nor destroy." The idea of peaceful cohabitation is clearly taken up in the citation; 65.25 repeats the statements about the wolf living with the lamb and the lion's diet of straw, summarizing the whole with the same promise of no harm or destruction. However, the assertion about the snake has changed. Now, instead of promising safe cohabitation, the citation promises humiliation. For that is the meaning of eating dust (cf. Mic. 7.17).

What is happening in the text here? Why has the author of the allusion changed course on this point? The decisive clue is probably found both in the replacement of "asp" and "viper" with "snake" (nḥš), and in the statement that he will eat "dust" (ʿpr). It is probable that what has happened here is that when the author of 65.25 went to cite 11.6-9 he also drew from Gen. 3.14 where God curses the "snake" (nḥš) to a diet of "dust" (ʿpr). Besides Isa. 65.25 and Mic. 7.17, Gen. 3.14 is the only other statement of this sort in the entire Hebrew Bible. Moreover, Mic. 7.17 differs from both Isa. 65.25 and Gen. 3.14 in that it compares the shame of the nations to a snake licking dust, whereas both the others make claims about the snake itself, who eats it. Thus, Genesis is a more probable point of influence on Isaiah at this point than is Micah. It is probable that the author of 65.25 would have had access to, or been aware of, Genesis 3, since he was writing in the post-exilic period, the time by which Genesis had likely reached its final form. The association of 11.6-9 with Genesis 3 would have been an easy one for the author of 65.25 to make, both because 11.6-9 depicts an Edenic state, and because his own vision of the future was clearly influenced by the very themes that appear in the early chapters of Genesis. Hence, he speaks of a "new heavens and new earth" wherein people will live supernaturally long lives (65.17-22).

If this is correct, then we may ask: why has the author of 65.25 conflated a citation of 11.6-9 with an allusion to Gen. 3.14? It is likely that he did so as a form of exegesis. He achieved a sort of exegetical synthesis through the dual allusion in 65.25. That is, having identified the "asp" and "viper" of Isa. 11.6-9 with the "snake" of Gen. 3.14 and holding that the curse of Gen. 3.14 would remain in effect, he produced a new textual blend that would suggest these exegetical conclusions to the reader. In this scenario, an earlier Isaianic oracle is read alongside another authoritative text, and the heavy lifting of theological synthesis is already accomplished for the reader who only needs to draw the desired inferences already encoded in the text. In the light of this point and our above discussion, it is not impossible that also underlying 65.25 is the earliest association between a future Davidic king and the curse of the snake, an association that comes into full bloom in later exegetical tradition (cf. Rev. 12.7-17).

Many additional examples of Isaianic allusion to other biblical texts could be cited. In Isa. 11.11–12.6, for example, one finds a technique typical of DI wherein the future restoration of Israel is proclaimed in terms of the Exodus story (Fishbane 1985: 355–356), including a direct citation of the Song of the Sea (compare Exod. 15.1 to Isa. 12.2, 5). Or, one could note the way in which the author of Isaiah 58–59 recasts statements from Deuteronomy to make the point that the salvation his hearers awaited was delayed by their sin, and would only come when they sought to care for those in need (compare Deut. 32.9-11 to Isa. 58.11-14, and Deut. 28–29 to Isa. 59.8-10 — on which see Sommer 1998: 134–135, 139). Examples could easily be multiplied (see Hibbard 2006, Lau 1994). Isaiah also alludes to literary traditions beyond the borders of Israel, interacting with Ancient Near Eastern textual culture more broadly (Hays 2008, Hutton 2007). However, at this point we should conclude our discussion of allusion in Isaiah by simply noting that the literary approach has done a great service in drawing attention to this feature of the text.

c. Narrative

It is probably fair to say that, of all the genres in the Bible, narrative has attracted the most attention from the literary approach (e.g. Alter 1981, Gunn 2000, Sternberg 1985). A brief glance at the indices of these works reveals that they give short shrift to Isaiah in considering the topic of narrative. Yet this prophetic book employs narrative to recount some of the most pivotal moments in the prophet's career, not to mention the careers of the Davidic kings he was sent to instruct. Isaiah 6 narrates the prophet's vision of God with his attendant Seraphim, reporting his grim commission and its place in the divine plan to produce a holy remnant. Isaiah 7 recounts how the prophet went to king Ahaz with a word of divine assurance when Jerusalem faced the peril of foreign invasion from the Syro-Ephraimite coalition. Likewise Isaiah 36–39 tells how he spoke a reassuring word to Hezekiah when Jerusalem faced a similar threat from a different enemy, the mighty Assyrians. Both events are pivotal to the ministry of Isaiah and to the prophetic oracles in the book. And both events are given narrative form. There is also a thin layer of narrative present in the prose of Isa. 20.1-6, a brief account of Isaiah's sign-act against Egypt. So clearly, narrative is key to the book's message, to how it weaves its pattern of meaning. The scholarly neglect of the Isaianic narratives is puzzling, for they are not impoverished as regards their form. Rather, they reflect the techniques of Hebrew narrative every bit as much as the patriarchal stories in Genesis, or the court tales of king David.

The literary analysis of biblical narrative has revealed an impressive sophistication woven into the fabric of these seemingly simple stories. This sophistication involves the deployment of an array of techniques, about which we will have more to say in the following chapters. Here it is sufficient to note that, above all, such analyses remind us that

> narrative is a *form of representation*. Abraham in Genesis is not a real person any more than a painting of an apple is a real fruit. This is not a judgment on the existence of a historical Abraham any more than it is a statement about the existence of apples. It is just that we should not confuse a historical individual with his narrative representation (Berlin 1983: 13).

This point is especially important to remember in the book of Isaiah. For, in seeking to understand the Isaianic narratives, we are not so much after what Isaiah, Hezekiah, or Ahaz did in history — however we might reconstruct that — as we are interested in seeing how these figures are represented in the narratives, what techniques are employed to give them depth — moral, psychological, spiritual, political, or other — and to what ends they are so characterized. While this example relates to characterization, the point is applicable to the whole range of techniques employed by the narrative form.

The single most important implication of the distinction between *historical reconstruction* and *narrative representation* noted by Berlin is that the reader should be careful not to import from elsewhere knowledge that we might have about the events and inject that into their portrayal in Isaiah. The Isaianic portrayal looks the way it does for a reason. Its narratives selectively tell their stories, for example, by leaving out parts that might distract from their point.

This can be illustrated by considering Isa. 7.1-17, the narrative recounting Isaiah's ministry to king Ahaz, and Ahaz's negative reaction to the prophetic word during the Syro-Ephraimite advance against Jerusalem. In this narrative, Ahaz is depicted in a negative light, being criticized by the prophet (v. 13). What was he criticized for? Historical reconstructions answer that Ahaz appealed to the Assyrians for help against the Syro-Ephraimite coalition. This has then been read into Isaiah 7 by several commentators (e.g. Clements 1980: 85, Seitz 1993: 77). Historically, this is an entirely plausible, if not probable, answer. The evidence does suggest that Ahaz appealed to Assyria for help against the Syro-Ephraimite aggressors (so 2 Kgs 16.7). And, moreover, such an appeal runs directly counter to the prophet's divine warning elsewhere against reliance on other nations (e.g. Isa. 20.1-6).

Indeed, Ahaz's appeal to Assyria clearly ran counter to the ideology of the Kings author as well (2 Kgs 16.1-20). In the Kings account, Ahaz's reliance on Assyria, which did indeed deliver Judah from the aggressors, led him to refashion the altar in the Lord's temple to look like that in the temple in Damascus (ironically, the capital of Syria). That this was a great sin in the eyes of the Kings author is clear because he prefaces the whole account with, Ahaz "did not do what was right in the sight of the Lord his God" (vv. 2-3). The account goes into great detail about the extensive measures Ahaz took in transforming the altar of the Lord's temple to reflect the pattern of the one in Damascus. To make his point, the author frames the whole account with two notes, each drawing a direct causal link between Ahaz's apostasy and his reliance upon the king of Assyria. The account begins, "When King Ahaz went to Damascus to meet King Tiglath-pileser of Assyria, he saw the altar that was at Damascus" (v. 10). After recounting how this led Ahaz to fashion an identical altar in Judah, the account simply ends with, "He did this because of the king of Assyria" (v. 18).

If the author of Isa. 7.1-17 was even remotely aware of this account (as he seems to have been [compare Isa. 7.1 with 2 Kgs 16.5]), then he would no doubt have been tempted to include it in his own narrative. He would have been tempted to do so, if not for historical accuracy, then because it would have provided further support for his condemnation of Ahaz's response to the divine word. But the author does not include the information from Kings. In the Isaiah account, it is only Ahaz's refusal to ask for the sign which justifies condemnation (vv. 12-13). In the Isaiah narrative, Ahaz is not censured for his appeal to Assyria, or even his unorthodox alteration of the Lord's altar. These are not even mentioned. Rather, he is censured for his refusal to ask for a sign that would confirm the divine promise of deliverance. And that is a very different justification. Thus, the author of Isaiah resisted the temptation of saying all that might be said about the incident, instead focusing his words, *and therefore the reader's attention*, on the point of his story, Ahaz's response to the divine command to seek a "sign." By omitting the appeal to Assyria, the author of Isaiah 7 focuses the reader on the "sign" and the crucial role it plays in the unfortunate incident.

Indeed, the first ten verses of the story lead up to Ahaz's refusal to request the sign. Verses 1-2 recount the threat and the fear this caused in "the house of David." Verses 3-9 then tell how Isaiah was sent to Ahaz to assure him that the attack would not succeed. This word of assurance concludes in v. 9 with a choice given Ahaz as representative of that house. "Unless you (pl.) believe, you (pl.) will not be established." Then, immediately following this, none other than God himself tells Ahaz to request a sign confirming the divine word just given, a request which Ahaz refuses, bringing divine displeasure on "the house of David" (vv. 10-13). To the divine imperative "ask" comes the response "I will not ask." Since the command to ask for a sign follows immediately on the warning that he must "believe," a direct connection is formed between Ahaz's lack of faith in the prophetic word and his refusal to ask for a sign. The sign was to confirm a *divine* promise — the Syro-Ephraimite aggressors will not prevail over the Davidic house – so that Ahaz's refusal to request that sign amounted to a lack of faith in *God*; it was a rejection of the warning in Isa. 7.9. Ahaz explains his refusal as an unwillingness to "test" God, a rationale which, in the light of the fact that it is God himself who commands him to ask for the sign, is at best irrelevant and at worst unbelief masquerading itself as piety. Thus, Ahaz's "pious" objection notwithstanding, the shape of the narrative forces us to conclude that to reject the sign-command is to not "believe." This lack of faith in the *divine* commitment to the Davidic house, thematized through the word "sign," emerges as the focal point of the first half of the story.

The "sign" remains at the center of the reader's attention in what follows. In the remainder of the narrative, the consequences of Ahaz's refusal play out in the form of a double-edged promise confirmed by a "sign" (vv. 14-17). Despite (and maybe because of) Ahaz's recalcitrance, a sign is given anyways. But now rather than simply affirming the entirely positive assurance found in vv. 3-9, this sign cuts both ways. Positively, the sign assures that the Syro-Ephraimite aggressors will be defeated (v. 16). Negatively, it promises an even greater threat in the future, the threat of Assyria who itself would eventually wreak havoc on Judah (v. 17, and v. 15 seen in the light of v. 22). Thus, while the first half of the narrative draws attention to Ahaz's lack of faith displayed in his refusal to ask for a sign, the second half draws out the future consequences of this failure through the giving of a sign. In this light, it is clear that the author places the "sign" — and therefore the divine plan — at the center of the narrative.

In the final chapter of our book we will see that he did this because the narrative of Ahaz in ch. 7 is inextricably bound to that of Hezekiah in chs. 36–39. In 36–39, the prophetic "sign" again plays a central role in the response of the Davidic house to foreign threat, this time to Assyrian invasion. The point of our present discussion, however, is that, if one injects information from the Kings account into the Isaiah version, then one will likely lose sight of the narrative's focus — the divine "sign" — and as a consequence overlook the role this plays in connecting the story to the Hezekiah narrative in creating a larger pattern of meaning in the book.

If as readers we import information into the narrative from our historical reconstruction of the incident, then we run the risk of missing the point of the Isaianic author, his emphasis on the faith of Ahaz in relation to the "sign." This is not to say that it is wrong to blend the two accounts in the interests of historical reconstruction, but simply that this should not substitute for reading the narrative along the lines given by its author. To do otherwise is bad reading. There is thus a real need to be clear about which questions we are asking and what methods are most likely to get us the answers we are looking for.

3. Conclusion

To sum up, a literary approach is at root a discourse-oriented approach, in that it seeks to make sense of the patterns of meaning found in the text, rather than inquire into the realities behind it, an interest belonging to source-oriented analysis. Moreover, if there was any doubt to begin with, it should be clear by now that Isaiah is a piece of literature; it displays all of the usual literary features that scholars find elsewhere in the Bible. Thus, as a literary text, it merits a literary approach. And as we saw in the introduction to this chapter, literary approaches to Isaiah invariably have at their heart an interest in reading the book holistically — even if it is made up of fragments from different authors. This idea of a holistic reading will be dealt with in the next chapter.

Chapter 5

Reading Isaiah Holistically

1. The Basis of a Holistic Reading

The last chapter sought to give an account of what a literary approach might entail. It also surveyed a number of features of Isaiah that are decidedly literary, leading to the conclusion that since Isaiah is a literary text, we are justified in taking a literary approach to it. And as was also noted in that chapter, the literary approach to Isaiah has at its center a holistic reading. The desire to read a text holistically flows naturally from a literary approach, since this approach is grounded in the discourse-oriented task of seeking meaningful coherence in a text's final form. To put it again in Sternberg's words: "Discourse-oriented analysis . . . sets out to understand not the realities behind the text but the text itself as a pattern of meaning and effect" (1985: 15). A holistic approach seeks to understand the textual part in the light of the whole, and the textual whole in the light of its parts. Literary readings with this holistic focus have been offered for the book as a whole (Webb 1990), as well as for sub-collections within it (Exum 1979). As was noted in the last chapter, these readings do not necessarily assume that the book of Isaiah was all written by a single author. In fact, most of them accept the standard view that the book is composite, being the work of many different hands.

But if the book is composite, then is it not simply an anthology, a collection of independent oracles, or a collection of collections? And if it is merely an anthology, then does that not invalidate reading it as a single book? We have seen that it was at one time common for scholars to argue that chs. 1–39 and chs. 40–66 developed entirely independently from one other, in effect constituting two separate books. This view raised the question as to how and why these two independent works were combined. As Williamson puts it, the most common explanation was "the conjecture that the combination was due to purely material considerations — the need to fill a complete and precious scroll by combining two shorter works into something approximately the same length as Jeremiah, Ezekiel, and the 'book' of the twelve minor prophets" (1994: 4). In this view, the book of Isaiah is no more than a mere folder full of unrelated documents: the reader should not expect to find coherence in the one any more than in the other. While this explanation for the joining of 1–39 with 40–66 was never found very satisfying, the issue of coherence remains. Even if 40–66 were written in the light of 1–39 (as many now maintain), Isaiah remains a composite work. And if Isaiah is composite, a collection of sorts, how does a holistic reading of it justify itself? What grounds are there for reading a collection as a single book?

a. Reader-response Criticism as a Basis for Holistic Reading

Many literary approaches to Isaiah appeal to the role of readers in "constructing" meaning as a basis for their own reading of the book (or a passage within it) as a meaningful whole. Such approaches usually transgress boundaries set up by earlier historical-critical approaches (Conrad 1991, Darr 1994, Exum 1979). This focus on the role of the reader has its theoretical basis in "reader-response," or "reader-oriented" criticism, a form of criticism construed in different ways by biblical scholars.

As applied to Isaiah, a central tenet of this critical method is to shift focus from the role of the author to that of the reader. Hence, Conrad argues,

> The locus of meaning with authorial intention is at considerable variance with contemporary literary theory, which is increasingly locating meaning in the process of reading . . . The reader, rather than being a passive receiver of a text communicating its meaning, is an active agent in making texts speak. The author is seen to lose active control of meaning and recedes into the background (1991: 1).

Having concluded this, Conrad sets out to understand the structure of the whole book, the repeated features that give "cohesion" to that structure, and finally the interaction of this structure with the reader *implied* in the text itself. The relevance of authorial intention having been dismissed, the composite nature of the book becomes irrelevant to Conrad's endeavor. It does not really matter how many authors stand behind Isaiah's final form, because the focus is on the reader.

In a similar but by no means identical approach, Darr suggests that scholars have appealed to literary methods out of frustration with the "atomistic and speculative tendencies of historical-critical methods" (1994: 13). Historical criticism traditionally forbade reading the first part of Isaiah with the second, because it saw the two as separate works. However, employing the newer literary approach focusing on the role of the reader, Darr argues that scholars may begin to ponder how to read the book as a whole. Indeed, though she acknowledges much recent redaction-critical work suggesting Isaiah was to be understood as in some sense a whole, she nevertheless focuses on the reader's construal of the text, explaining her reasoning as follows: "because readers themselves play a role in actualizing texts . . . we must leave open the possibility that they discern relationships between texts not, consciously or unconsciously, in the redactors' thoughts" (1994: 22). Thus, in her view a reader-oriented approach becomes detached from the work of authors or editors. Her specific aim is to discern how a first-time reader in the post-exilic period would have encountered the book sequentially. She seeks to illuminate this by tracing female and child imagery through the book from the first chapter to the last.

Reader-oriented approaches to Isaiah often argue that, because all we have is a single book called Isaiah, this book — rather than speculatively reconstructed sources — constitutes the reading context. The reader encounters Isaiah as a single whole, not as so many sources.

In response to this form of holistic reading grounded in reader-response criticism, we may recall our discussion in the previous chapter, where it was noted that an awareness of the role of the reader need not lead to a neglect of the intentions of the author. The role of the reader and that of the author are cogently held together by Sternberg who argues for a model that seeks "to make sense of the discourse in terms of communication, always goal-directed on the speaker's part and always requiring interpretive activity on the addressee's" (1985: 15). Thus, it is hardly necessary to view the problem through the "either/or" lens of an approach like Conrad's.

To develop this point, I would note that, although such reader-response approaches to Isaiah make no claim to detecting authorial intention, the readings they produce are often worth considering from this perspective. For example, Conrad observes several parallels between the narratives of Isaiah 7 and 36–39 (1991: 36–40) which suggest that the author of this material sought deliberately to contrast king Ahaz with his successor Hezekiah. He also observes some obvious links between the first chapter of the book and its last two (1991: 102), which suggest a conscious attempt to give the whole book shape. Indeed, much of what Conrad says about the structure of Isaiah was anticipated by scholars for whom these features were obvious signs of deliberate editorial shaping. Hence, Ackroyd (1987) saw the contrast between Ahaz and Hezekiah as deliberate; and long before it had become fashionable to draw conclusions of this kind regarding the literary shape of Isaiah, Liebreich argued that the parallels between chs. 1 and 65–66 suggest the "intention and fixed determination to make the Book end in the same vein with which it begins" (1956: 276). That Conrad should build on their observations while dismissing the importance of their appeals to editorial/authorial intention only seems to strengthen the point that reader-oriented approaches like his often contain observations which receive a satisfying explanation by appeal to intention. Such structural features suggest that the book *has been given* meaningful shape, that it has been interwoven with clues to help the attentive reader discover larger patterns of meaning.

b. Redaction Criticism as a Basis for Holistic Reading

While these scholars ground a holistic reading in the role of the reader in "constructing" meaning, others ground it in the role of the redactor in constructing texts. Recent redaction-critical work on Isaiah, perhaps under the influence of literary approaches, has given new attention to the role of redactors in creating literary works with meaningful shape. They were not mere collectors. Rather, they were like those who in modern times edit raw footage into coherent movies, carefully considering each juxtaposition and every splice. As a consequence, the reader of their work may expect to find a great deal more cohesion and coherence than was previously thought. This view of the biblical redactor as a skilled author of sorts has been contrasted with the older view of the compiler by Barton.

> Against more sophisticated types of redaction criticism, which share with modern literary approaches an attachment to finding unity and closure in the finished form of books, the older style of historical criticism represented by source analysis treats the biblical books we now have as put together without great skill from pre-existing fragments or longer continuous sources which have been broken up into smaller sections . . . The compilers of biblical books were not trying to produce 'works' in the literary sense, with a clear theme or plot and a high degree of closure, but rather anthologies of material which could be dipped into at any point (1998: 6).

The elevated estimation of the biblical redactor in recent scholarship over against the older view of him as simply a compiler (if this characterization is generally correct) may owe itself to two converging trends in scholarship. First, as we have already suggested, this may be due to the rise of literary approaches in biblical scholarship. These literary approaches have been very successful in sensitizing biblical scholars to the possibility of finding patterns of meaning in texts, even when those texts are still regarded as composite. Indeed, in an early and very influential book on the literary approach to the Bible, Alter held these two facets of the text together, literary artistry on the one hand and sources on the other (1981: 19–20). Thus, he cites approvingly the even older study of Rosenberg (1975 citation from Alter), who argued,

> It may actually improve our understanding of the Torah to remember that it is *quoting* documents, that there is, in other words, a purposeful documentary *montage* that must be perceived as a unity, regardless of the number and types of smaller units that form the building blocks of its composition. Here, the weight of literary interest falls upon the activity of the *final* redactor, whose artistry requires far more careful attention than it has hither to been accorded.

Rosenberg was responding to some of the then new literary approaches to the Bible, arguing that the lessons of historical criticism — namely, the discovery of the composite nature of many biblical books — should not be ignored, but rather incorporated into this newer approach. What is striking about the quote is that already in 1975 we find the linking of the literary approach to a call to show more attention to the artistry of the redactor, all under the rubric of "the *final* redactor." Because a focus on the final redactor has become the watchword of much redaction-critical work since, we may suppose that Rosenberg was expressing then a broader sentiment regarding the skill of the redactor, one that arose in connection with the literary approach.

The second trend which could have contributed to the reassessment of the skill of the redactor is the general shift in interest from the origins to the later representation of all things biblical. While the interest in "origins" continues unabated, there has been a noticeable increase of interest in the later periods of biblical history. Thus, where much effort was put into uncovering the prophets themselves — their political roles, their psychologies, their messages — there is now also a strong interest in how these prophets came to be represented in the prophetic literature whose final form is often quite late (Ackroyd 1978, Childs 1979: 306–310). Thus, where older generations of scholars would discard redaction as later accretion irrelevant to uncovering the historical prophet, recent scholarship has given renewed attention to this redaction and the way it construes the prophet and his message. I would venture to suggest that this too has led to a more sensitive appraisal of the work of the redactor than it had hither to been given.

Whatever the reason, there has been a general reappraisal of the skill and artistry of the redactor, and this has certainly changed assessments of the book of Isaiah. Where before it was thought that Isaiah was the product of mere compilation, it is now widely recognized that the book arose from carefully considered redaction. At different stages of Isaiah's formation, redactors sought to bring a degree of coherence to the collection, shaping it in various ways to create patterns of meaning. It is perhaps telling that Barton considers this redactional reappraisal of Isaiah under the heading of "Literary Readings of Isaiah." He describes this reappraisal and its consequences for reading Isaiah as follows.

> the disparate material from which the work is composed have . . . been drawn together in such a way that the resulting book is much more than a collection of fragments — the whole is greater than the sum of its parts. By paying attention to the subtleties of the text, it is possible, and desirable, to read Isaiah as a unity. Taken together, and with the order imposed on them by the redactors, all the oracles attributed to Isaiah 'make sense': they are a book, not a mere folder full of rough drafts and collected scraps (1995: 107).

It is clear from this quote that this redactional reappraisal of Isaiah has opened the door to holistic readings of the book. The redactors are thought to have put clues into the book that would help the reader get the "big picture."

2. Isaiah as "Anthology" and as "Book"

It is a consequence of what has just been said that any notion of a holistic reading of Isaiah will surely have to probe more deeply into what it might mean that Isaiah is a "unity." To do so, we will need to consider the very different ideas of Isaiah as "anthology" on the one hand and Isaiah as "book" on the other. Whereas "book" implies a tightly knit unity, "anthology" suggests a loosely related compilation.

As we have seen throughout this study, the formation of the book began with Isaiah the prophet and ended in the post-exilic period at the earliest, spanning more than two centuries. Since this will mean that multiple authors and redactors were involved in the process which gave us the book, the book itself will contain many discrete intentions. If Isaiah reflects many intentions, then isn't it just an anthology, rather than a single book?

This way of putting the issue presents a false alternative in light of how books like Isaiah were made in ancient Israel. Isaiah is a sort of anthology, a collection of collections, and as such contains many rough edges. But that need not imply that the book is bereft of any literary shape, or meaningful coherence, that there are no larger patterns of meaning to guide the reader. In fact, just the opposite appears to be the case.

a. The Redeployment of Older Literary Structures by Later Editors

To begin with, it is often the case in Isaiah that later editors did not merely preserve older sources alongside their own fresh contributions; rather, they sought to coordinate their own contributions with the earlier sources. They built on the older literary structures, developing the older intentionalities through new literary strategies. These later editors can be compared to builders who are tasked with constructing a new home on a pre-existing foundation which they themselves did not make. They must build that new structure on that pre-existing foundation. While the house they build will therefore be defined in many ways by that foundation, it will nevertheless be of their own making, reflecting their own creativity and strategic choices (cf. Seitz 1988). In previous chapters I have already noted several examples where earlier sources have been redeployed in new literary strategies.

In one such instance, Isa. 63.7–64.12 preserves a lament wherein the voice complains to God that, among other things, Jerusalem and its temple had been destroyed by foreign oppressors. The lament certainly stems from after the Babylonian destruction, and may have been composed for recitation at the site of the ruined temple (cf. Psalm 106; Neh. 9.6-37; see Blenkinsopp 2003: 257–266 and Williamson 1990). Whatever its original setting and function, however, this lament is now incorporated into the book of Isaiah. And the hand which incorporated it was likely that which wrote 65–66, chapters which immediately follow this lament. What suggests this is the fact that 65–66 were written as a direct response to the complaint of the lament (this was discussed on p. 46 above). Where the lament asks concerning the destroyed city and temple, "will you restrain yourself over this, will you be silent?" (64.12), God responds that quite the contrary he has sought his people, but they rejected him, prompting him to respond in judgment: "I will not keep silent, but I will repay" (65.1-6). While the response is critical to the lament, it is also attentive to its request. Hence, where the lament pleads "return on account of your servants" (63.17), God promises "I will act on account of my servants" (65.9), the only difference being that in the latter passage these servants are a holy remnant whereas in the former they are all the people. Thus, what was likely an older source composed for an entirely different function has been incorporated into the book and built upon for the purpose of forming a new literary strategy, one that sought to address the very real issues raised in the lament while at the same time justifying God against charges of silence toward his people (Stromberg 2010: 30–32).

Isaiah 56.1 furnishes another instance where sources have been incorporated into a larger literary strategy. In this instance, however, the scope of that strategy is much broader. As discussed earlier (pp. 41–42), Rendtorff (1993) convincingly shows that the author of 56.1 has combined PI's conception of "righteousness/salvation" ($\d{s}^e d\bar{a}q\hat{a}$) with DI's use of this term. Both parts of the book define the meaning of $\d{s}^e d\bar{a}q\hat{a}$ by placing it parallel to another term. PI pairs "righteousness" with the word "judgment" ($mi\check{s}p\bar{a}\d{t}$) several times, but DI never does. DI frequently associates it with words from the root $y\check{s}^c$ ("salvation, to save," etc.), an association not found in PI. However, 56.1 combines both pairs, a combination not found in the book before this. In combining these terms in 56.1, this later author has drawn the two earlier parts of the book together into a single strategy which emphasizes the importance of doing "righteousness" as a basis for inheriting "salvation." The implication of Rendtorff's study is that the author of TI sought to coordinate the sources he inherited, namely PI and DI, into a single literary strategy. The author of TI built his own work on the foundation of the intentions and strategies of his sources.

Another example of this would be Isaiah 36–39, the narrative recounting the Assyrian siege of Jerusalem, Hezekiah's reaction to it, and divine deliverance from it. In the final chapter of our book we will see that this narrative was lifted from 2 Kgs 18.13–20.19 and reshaped in such a way as to contribute to a larger literary strategy in the book that also involved ch. 7. In Isaiah there are many other examples where a source has been built upon and incorporated into a larger literary strategy in the book, but the point seems clear enough. Just because Isaiah is a collection does not mean it is a mere anthology; there are signs that the collection has been given a great deal of shape.

Of course, when an editor incorporated a source such as 36–39 into the literary strategy he was developing, he may not have viewed every feature of that source as equally relevant to his purpose. In a composite document like Isaiah, we should expect to find some loose ends, some intentionalities embedded in the earlier sources which are left undeveloped by the new purpose to which they were put. Because Isaiah is multi-layered in this way, we should not expect that every single literary move now preserved in the book will have contributed to a larger strategy. That said, in the face of the above evidence, it seems wholly appropriate that we should expect to find broader strategies in the book, strategies put there by authors who wished to guide readers in their understanding of the material, strategies which were to generate larger patterns of meaning.

b. The Divine Inspiration of the Older Isaianic Oracles for the Book's Later Editors

There is another reason why the book of Isaiah, though being a diverse collection of oracles, would have nevertheless cohered for those involved in its formation, and this too suggests that calling the book a mere anthology without any further overarching coherence fails to do justice to the nature of its composition. It can scarcely be doubted that driving the latest stages of Isaiah's composition was the conviction that the older Isaianic oracles stemmed from the same God who was at work in inspiring the new word.

To take one example, the author of TI likely identified that divine voice speaking in oracles from Isaiah of Jerusalem with that voice found in DI, and it was this same voice for which he regarded himself a spokesman. This, it seems to me, is the most obvious explanation for the fact that he cites the earlier oracles in an authoritative way *and* preserves them in the process of adding his own fresh work at the end. For instance, note how he cites 11.6-9, and adds "says the Lord" (65.25, on which see pp. 67–70). Note also how he builds his own oracle in 57.14-21 on allusions to chs. 6 and 40, concluding the saying with "there is no peace for the wicked *says my God*" (on this passage see pp. 49–50).

This conviction — that the same divine voice lay behind Isaianic oracles of differing provenance and authorship — was probably not limited to TI. It was probably operative in other stages of the formation of the book as well — in attaching DI to an early form of PI (which had inspired the author of DI), in the juxtaposition of oracles from different periods, and in ultimately associating the whole with Isaiah of Jerusalem who is presented as the divine spokesman, the prophet of God (cf. Seitz 1998: 168–193). Above all else, then, it was this conviction of divine origin that gave the book its "unity" for its later editors and authors. Since they were the ones ultimately responsible for the book's final form, their assumption of divine unity will inevitably have made itself felt in the composition.

3. A Single Divine Plan Underlying Isaiah's Historically Divergent Material

Perhaps as a consequence of this, the later redactors of the book, gazing over the historically diverse material bequeathed to them, will have seen

the same God at work throughout the different periods covered in the
mass of oracles they inherited and sought to shape into a book (Seitz
1991, Williamson 1994: 94–115). It will have been the same God guid-
ing Israel's destiny in the Syro-Ephraimite crisis (chs. 7–8) that was at
work in the Assyrian crisis (chs. 36–38) and return from Babylonian exile
(chs. 40–55). This God will have been involved in the events of the life of
his people in the post-exilic period as well (chs. 56–66). These moments
in Israel's history were preserved in the oracles inherited by the later
redactors. Since they believed that it was the same God at work in each
of these events, it was perhaps inevitable that they should have regarded
them as interconnected instances of a single divine plan. Childs captures
this thought well.

> From the perspective of the events of 587, of the exile, and of the rise of the
> Medes and Persians, the significance of Israel's history in reference to the world
> powers of Assyria and Babylon was interpreted retrospectively as consisting of
> the one theological purpose of God with his people (2000: 116).

Given that the post-exilic editors of the book believed one God was at
work in all of these events, it is difficult to see how else they would have
construed the oracles they inherited which were tied to these events and
which they regarded as divinely inspired. In a very broad sense, the whole
book of Isaiah can be seen as a sequence: PI contains the only Assyrian
period material which is followed by DI wherein a Babylonian setting
gives way to Persian rule which is then presupposed in TI. In view of
this, it is not unreasonable to suppose that such a unitary view of history
sought to give the book a sequence wherein the Assyrian period gives way
to the Babylonian which then gives way to the Persian — all in a manner
not dissimilar to the view underlying the statue in Daniel 2 which tells of
the kingdoms that would rise and fall before the establishment of God's
own kingdom. Apart from this rather general observation, however,
I would note that there are specific literary strategies woven into the
book which reflect later attempts at coordinating the various events into
a single plan of God — i.e. retrospective interpretations at the level of
redaction.

One such strategy can be traced on the basis of a cluster of key terms.
As many have noted, biblical authors and editors often employed the
repetition of key words or phrases to develop literary strategies (e.g.
Alter 1981: 88–113). In the present instance, one can discern a strategy
of repetition designed to bring together into a single divine plan the events
of the Syro-Ephraimite war, the Assyrian crisis, and the fall of Babylon
with the subsequent return and restoration of the people. The key terms
employed work together to contrast the divine plan with the nefarious
plans of foreign nations: the main terms are "to plan" ($y^{c}ṣ$), "to stand"
(qwm), and "to frustrate" (prr). To this verbal core, several other terms and
phrases attach themselves at various points. Each of the passages involved
in this strategy owes either its final form or its inclusion into the book
to the end of the exile at the earliest (on ch. 7, which is now of a piece

with chs. 8–9, see pp. 15–16; on ch. 14 see pp. 16–18; on chs. 36–39 see p. 15). As a result, the strategy owes its full form to the post-exilic period (cf. Clements 1989).

The first passage to be considered is Isa. 7.1-17, which recounts how the Syro-Ephraimite coalition attacked Jerusalem and attempted to install in that city a king of their own liking. This threat overwhelmed the ruling "house of David" with fear, so that the prophet Isaiah was sent to offer the reigning king Ahaz assurances that this coalition would not prevail (vv. 1-3). Isaiah was to tell Ahaz not to "fear" the aggressors who had "devised a plan" (*y'ṣ*) against him, for their plan would not "stand" (*l' tqwm*) (vv. 5, 7). Then, Ahaz was told by God to request a "sign" as confirmation of this assurance. He refused (vv. 10-13). As a result, he was given the "sign" of the birth of a child named Immanuel ("God with us"). This sign did in fact promise the demise of the coalition (vv. 14-16), but it also signified an even greater threat — the invasion of Judah by "the king of Assyria" (v. 17). Thus, in this brief narrative we already see that two quite different moments in Israel's history have been brought together under a single divine plan: the Syro-Ephraimite war has seamlessly given way to the future Assyrian crisis, all in the moment of Ahaz's unfortunate decision.

For reasons we shall see below, it is significant that this whole sequence is framed in terms of its significance for the Davidic line. Hence, at the beginning of the narrative, it is "the house of David" that is told of the threat (v. 2). It was against the royal throne in Jerusalem that the "plan" was devised which would not "stand" (vv. 5-6). The assurance given Ahaz ends with an ultimatum that is clearly directed to the royal line more broadly, explaining why the verbs are plural, rather than singular: "If you (pl.) do not believe (*t'mynw*), you (pl.) will not be established (*t'mnw*)" (v. 9). The plural verbs indicate that the consequences of Ahaz's choice would redound to subsequent kings in his line. Moreover, as Barthel (1997: 169) notes, the wording of the ultimatum echoes the promise to David that his house and his kingdom would be "established" (*n'mn*) forever (2 Sam. 7.16). Finally, when Ahaz fails to believe by refusing to ask for a sign, he is told that God will bring the "king of Assyria" on "the house of your ancestor" (v. 17). It is sufficiently clear, then, that the "plan" devised against the throne would not "stand" because it ran up against the divine plan for the Davidic house which was to be established forever. Equally clear, however, is the future threat incurred against that house, again seemingly placing its future in jeopardy. What would Assyrian invasion mean for its future?

An answer comes swiftly in the very next chapter (Isaiah 8), which is of a piece with this narrative. Here, perhaps as a contrast to Ahaz's decision, Isaiah appoints "faithful" (*n'mnym*) witnesses for himself, and is told to write the name "Maher-shalal-hash-baz" on a tablet, the name of the child he would father with the prophetess. The name of this child was to signify the defeat of the Syro-Ephraimite coalition before the king of Assyria (8.1-4). Immediately following this brief narrative it is reported in vv. 5-9 that the Lord continued to speak to the prophet, threatening the following:

because the people had rejected "the gently flowing waters of Shiloh" by rejoicing over the kings of the Syro-Ephramite coalition, God was now bringing against them the "strong waters of the mighty river," the "king of Assyria" and "all his army." The king would overflow "Judah," filling the whole land. Thus, the Assyrian threat is reiterated, again raising the question about the fate of the house of David. What would Assyrian invasion mean for its future? On the heels of this grim announcement swiftly comes the answer in the form of a challenge to all the nations.

> Break forth, O peoples, and be shattered;
>> Give ear all far countries.
> Give ear and be shattered;
> Give ear and be shattered.
> Plan a plan ('ṣw 'ṣh), but it will be frustrated (tpr);
>> Speak a word, but it will not stand (l' yqwm).
>>> For God is with us (Immanuel). (8.9-10)

The placement of this passage immediately after the threat of Assyrian invasion is clearly deliberate. Hence, just as vv. 5-8 end with a reference to Immanuel ("God with us"), so too do vv. 9-10. In the latter, however, the name serves as the basis for deliverance — i.e. the frustration of the nations' "plans" against Judah (v. 10). Placing the promise of deliverance (vv. 9-10) immediately after the foretold doom (vv. 5-8) clearly seeks to mitigate the Assyrian threat. The plans of the Assyrians against Judah would not stand. And this brings us to the broader literary strategy being developed regarding the divine plan. In assuring deliverance from Assyria, vv. 9-10 promise that the nations' "plan" would not "stand," thereby echoing the previous narrative where precisely the same terms are used to describe the Syro-Ephraimite "plan" against Judah that would not "stand." Thus, just as the name of Immanuel was a sign in ch. 7 that the Syro-Ephraimite threat would be repelled, so now it is the basis for repelling the threat of the Assyrians, or indeed of any "far country" for that matter. Moreover, since the sign of Immanuel was so closely tied to the divine plan of the Davidic promise in ch. 7, we may suppose that something of the same logic is being applied here, only now to the Assyrian threat.

In saying that a clear strategy is being developed in these passages, I do not mean to imply that they were all written up at one time, only that the text was put together with an eye toward a deliberate strategy based on the key words "plan" and "stand," to which we can now add "frustrate." For one attempt to sort out the history of the development of these passages, see Clements (1989). Whatever the exact history of the text, we have seen thus far a clear strategy that has been woven into the text, a strategy which repeats key words to drive home the point that the "plans" of foreign nations will "not stand" and are destined to be "frustrated" when they come up against the divine plan tied to the house of David.

The next passage to be considered comes in Isa. 14.24-27, which, compared with 8.9-10, goes a step further by proclaiming the "breaking" of Assyria "in my land." The connection with our earlier passages is immediately apparent in the choice of vocabulary.

> The Lord of Hosts has sworn saying:
> Surely, just I purposed, so it will happen;
>> just as I planned (*y* ʿṣ*ty*), it will stand (*tqwm*)
> – to break Assyria in my land
>> and trample him on my mountains,
> so that his yoke will be removed from them,
>> and his burden from their shoulder.
> This is the plan (*h* ʿṣ*h*) that is planned (*hy* ʿwṣ*h*) against all the earth;
>> this is the hand that is outstretched against all the nations.
> For the Lord has planned (*y* ʿṣ), and who can frustrate (*ypr*) it?
>> His hand is outstretched, and who can turn it back? (14.24-27)

Here emerges a theme that could only be inferred by its opposite in the previous two passages. In both 7.1-17 and 8.9-10, the repeated terms focused on the "plans" of hostile nations that would not "stand," and it was largely by inference that we arrived at the conclusion that their plans would be "frustrated" because they ran up against the divine plan. What lay embedded in these earlier passages as an assumption is now explicitly stated in 14.24-25: "Surely, just I purposed, thus it will happen; just as I planned (*y* ʿṣ*ty*), it will stand (*tqwm*) — to break Assyria in my land and trample him on my mountains." Here it is explicitly stated that God has a "plan" that would "stand" and not be "frustrated." Assyria would not prevail over Israel because it was not in the divine plan.

In our discussion of both 7.1-17 and 8.9-10, it emerged that this divine plan derives from the promise to David that his kingdom would be established forever. In that light, it is obviously significant that the plan to "break" Assyria in ch. 14 has as its goal to remove its oppressive yoke from off the shoulder of the people: "his yoke will be removed from them, and his burden from their shoulder" (v. 25a). This phrase refers directly to the royal oracle of ch. 9 which announces that in connection with the birth of a child to the Davidic house the yoke of the oppressor would be shattered: "the yoke of their burden, the bar of their shoulder . . . you have broken" (v. 4). So confident was the writer of 14.25 that the reader would make this connection to ch. 9 that he did not even bother supplying an antecedent for "their" in "their shoulder" — a word which has a clear antecedent in ch. 9. In making this reference to the royal oracle, 14.24-27 aligns itself with the grounding of the divine plan found in 7.1-17 and 8.9-10. Like these two passages, 14.24-27 grounds God's "plan" to break Assyria and remove its oppressive yoke in a divine commitment to the royal house. The logic of this grounding emerges from the royal oracle itself, which concludes with a description of, and divine commitment to, the reign of the Davidic king.

> His authority shall grow continually, and there shall be endless peace for the throne of David and his kingdom. He will establish and uphold it with justice

and with righteousness from this time onward and forevermore. The zeal of the Lord of hosts will do this. (9.7 NRSV)

Any fulfillment of this divinely assured promise of Davidic rule necessitated that the foreign yoke be removed. It is therefore precisely this which God had "planned" and promised would "stand" in 14.24-25 — the removal of the Assyrian yoke. Further reinforcing the role of the Davidic promises in all of this, the language of these promises permeates 9.1-7 (cf. 2 Samuel 7, and see Williamson 1998: 35–37).

The grounding of 14.24-27 in 9.1-7 can be seen to have been prepared for by several further aspects of the literary strategy, particularly those found in ch. 10. The birth and naming of a child who would ultimately be associated with the overthrow of Assyria is not unique to 9.6. As we have seen, this is precisely the connection in which Immanuel is understood. The naming of both children is tied directly to the divine overthrow of Assyrian oppression in the present shape of the material. This was seen clearly in 8.9-10 which concludes with a reference to Immanuel ("God with us"). It is also evident in 10.19-27 which, through a series of references to 9.1-7, grounds the fall of Assyria in the royal oracle 9.1-7, and in particular in the naming of the child there. Isaiah 10.27 again refers to the removal of the burden and the yoke from the shoulder (cf. 9.4). Isaiah 10.26 again compares the overthrow to the smiting of "Midian" (cf. 9.4). The most significant reference to ch. 9 for our purposes comes in 10.21 where, in a play on the name given the child in 9.6, the promise is made that a remnant will return to El Gibbor ("the mighty God").

Given that the literary strategy draws such a strong parallel between Immanuel and the child born in ch. 9, it seems that we are to take them as one and the same person (cf. Clements 1996). This impression is strengthened by 10.19-27, which blends the above references to 9.1-7 with echoes of 7.1-17 and ch. 8, where Immanuel plays an important role. Isaiah 10.21-22 twice refers to Shear Yashub ("a remnant will return"), a name found in 7.3. And the "overflowing" righteousness of 10.22 probably plays on the Assyrian "overflowing" the land of Judah in 8.8.

Whatever the identity of these two children, the parallel drawn between them unmistakably prepares the way for the grounding of 14.24-27 in 9.1-7. Given that Assyria's failure is also grounded in the birth of a child in 8.9-10, the grounding of 14.24-27 in 9.1-7 appears quite natural from the point of view of the literary strategy to which all three passages belong. And given the key role $y^{c}ṣ$ ("to plan") plays in this strategy, this grounding may have been further secured by the other of the child's names, "Wonderful *Counselor* ($yw^{c}ṣ$)" (9.6). On the names, see Wegner (2009: 244–245).

There is therefore ample reason to conclude that in 14.24-27, as in 7.1-17 and 8.9-10, the nefarious plans of the nations against God's people would fail because they were opposed by a divine plan grounded in God's promise to David. Thus far, that plan spans the rise and fall of both the Syro-Ephraimite and Assyrian threats.

But what about the next event on the horizon of Isaiah's history,

Babylonian exile? Does this figure into the strategy we have been tracing? This question brings us to the second half of 14.24-27, which we have not yet discussed.

> This is the plan (h ʿšh) that is planned (hy ʿwṣh) against all the earth;
>   this is the hand that is outstretched against all the nations.
> For the Lord has planned (y ʿṣ), and who can frustrate (ypr) it?
>   His hand is outstretched, and who can turn it back? (14.26-27)

However these two verses came to be attached to the preceding two, it is clear that they seek to expand what was just said. The second half of the passage universalizes the divine plan aimed specifically at Assyria in vv. 24-25, extending it to "all the nations." As it is presented, this move is not merely a reapplication. Rather, Assyrian destruction is seen as part of a larger plan that involves all the nations. Assyria is an example of this plan. Hence, the second half begins "this [referring to Assyrian destruction] is the plan planned against *all the earth*." Assyrian destruction is seen as an instance of a much larger pattern of divine activity. It is obviously fitting, then, that 14.24-27 should stand near the front of the oracles against the nations in chs. 13–23. Indeed, precisely the language we have been tracing, language which saturates 14.24-27, is applied to Egypt in 19.11-17 and Tyre in 23.8-9. The first passage is especially noteworthy, since it contrasts the divine plan with the counsel of foreign nations, a contrast also developed in the above mentioned texts.

> The wise counselors (y ʿṣy) of Pharoah give stupid counsel (ʿṣh). Where now are your wise men? Let them tell you . . . what the Lord of Hosts has planned (y ʿṣ) against Egypt . . . On that day the land of Judah will become a terror to the Egyptians; everyone to whom it is mentioned will fear because of the plan (ʿṣh) that the Lord of Hosts is planning (yw ʿṣ) against them. (19.11-12, 16-17).

By reference to this repeated terminology, the oracles against Egypt and Tyre are subsumed into the larger pattern of divine activity. Egypt and Tyre become further instances of the divine plan against "all nations." But that still leaves us with the place of Babylon in this plan. How does this figure into the strategy we have been tracing?

From the point of view of the book of Isaiah, Babylonian exile will have been the biggest foreign yoke of all. It is therefore hardly a coincidence that the universalized saying against Assyria in 14.24-27 comes right after a lengthy oracle against Babylon (13.1–14.23), an oracle which has been made to stand at the head of the whole of the oracles against the nations, a position of prominence clearly warranted by its prominent place in Israel's history as a foreign oppressor. Since we have already seen that the divine plan in 14.24-27 is applied to other nations in this section, we may reasonably suppose that it will have been the basis for the oracle against Babylon as well. This supposition is strengthened considerably by the fact that 14.24-27 follows this oracle. Indeed, this short passage may have been partially composed in relation to the Babylonian oracle (Clements

1989). Be that as it may, the literary strategy seems clear enough. Through the inclusion of the Babylonian oracle at the head of this section and by its placement just before 14.24-27, the fall of Babylon becomes another instance of God's "plan" against "all nations." It too is subsumed within, and becomes an example of, a much larger pattern of divine activity.

If this is so, and because that "plan" had as its aim the removal of the yoke of the foreign oppressor, we would expect the oracle against Babylon to draw out the positive implications of the fall of that nation for God's people. Indeed, this is so. After announcing that a "signal" would be raised to indicate the destruction of Babylon (ch. 13), the positive implications of this destruction for exiled Israel are drawn out in 14.1-4. There it is said that, with the fall of Babylon, the nations would bring the people back to their land, and God would give them rest from the "toil" and "hard service" that they "had been forced to serve" in the exile, language whose thought clearly echoes the Assyrian "yoke" and "burden" to be removed in 14.24-25. Thus, the oracle against Babylon in 13.1–14.23 fits the pattern we have been tracing, the divine plan encoded in literary strategy.

There is only one remaining feature of this strategy that we have not yet seen in connection with the Babylonian oracle. Is the removal of the Babylonian yoke (with the accompanying return and restoration) also connected to the royal promises? The answer would appear to be yes, since the Babylonian oracle is now grounded in 14.24-27, which we saw above makes reference to the royal oracle in 9.1-7. This positive answer is strengthened by another component of Isaiah's composition that is clearly connected to the Babylonian oracle, namely, Isa. 11.1–12.6, the passage just before 13.1–14.23. Just like the Babylonian oracle, 11.1–12.6 also promises that a "signal" would be raised resulting in the nations bringing the exiled Israelites back to their land where they would enjoy restoration and freedom from foreign domination. And in 11.1–12.6, as we have come to expect from the strategy we have been tracing, this restoration is tied directly to a royal oracle (11.1-10) wherein none other than the king himself stands as the "signal" to the nations who were to return the people (Stromberg 2008).

To summarize the whole of our discussion, a single strategy employing a cluster of key terms ties together the Syro-Ephramite threat, the Assyrian crisis, and the fall of Babylon into a single divine plan grounded in the promises to David. One divine thread has been made to hold all of these events together in a theologically meaningful sequence. There are certainly other passages which could have been mentioned as part of this strategy. Isaiah 36–39, for instance, deliberately contrasts Hezekiah with Ahaz, establishing a link between the Syro-Ephraimite and Assyrian crises. At the same time, this narrative forecasts the Babylonian destruction, so that all three moments are again held together in a single divine plan. And here too that plan is grounded in the promises to David. Hence, the oracle assuring Hezekiah that the Assyrians would be defeated (37.22-35) makes reference to 9.1-7 ("the zeal of the Lord of Hosts will do this" [9.7//37.32]), and it concludes with this explanation: "I will defend this city to save it for my sake and *for the sake of my servant David.*" As Barton has argued in the light of 36–39, the editors of prophetic books were concerned with "the pattern of divine activity which all historical events revealed" (1995: 96).

There are other literary strategies in Isaiah that signal temporal transitions in the divine plan, most notably the contrast developed in DI between the "former things" and "new things" — a contrast which was to signal the transition from the period of judgment (Babylonian exile) to the time of salvation (return and restoration under the Persian king Cyrus) (Haran 1963, North 1950). While space does not permit a discussion of this here, it is noteworthy in the light of what was just said that the author of DI seems to have drawn on the royal oracle in Isaiah 9 (especially its first verse) in developing this theme (Gosse 1996, Williamson 1993). Indeed, DI ends with a clear reference to the Davidic promises, offering to those who would listen a renewal of the "eternal covenant, the sure (*n'mnym*) mercies of David" (55.3). In view of the fact that the "former things" are linked to the downfall of Babylon in DI where they are seen as having been announced beforehand (see especially ch. 48), it is probably also significant that several scholars have argued for a connection with Isaiah 13–14 which we just examined (Childs 1979: 330, Seitz 2001a: 356). If both references are correct, DI may be picking up where the earlier strategy left off, projecting the divine plan beyond the fall of Babylon and into the Persian period.

These examples clearly reflect later literary strategies woven into the book, strategies which seek to coordinate various events into a single plan of God. It emerges from these instances that a key turning point in this plan was the exile to Babylon and the subsequent hope of return and restoration. This would have been a natural point of interest to the book's latest editors since they lived in the aftermath of this event and continued to look forward to the brighter day that was to follow (see, e.g., chs. 58–60). Indeed, as was seen in the first three chapters of this study, the exile and the subsequent hope for restoration became a central lens through which the later redactors of the book presented the Isaianic oracles bequeathed to them. Since every major section of the book has been made to reflect this key turning point in the divine plan, it emerges as a central ingredient in Isaiah's "pattern of meaning," its literary strategy. Of course this conclusion need not imply that all of these passages were added by a single hand. We noted above, for instance, that there is every reason to believe that later editors of the book built on the work of their predecessors, redeploying older sources in newer strategies.

It is only natural that this conviction of a divine plan connecting the different events recounted in Isaiah should have turned the editors' attention to the future. From their post-exilic point of view, the Syro-Ephraimite threat, the Assyrian crisis, the Babylonian exile, and even the return to the land all lay in the past (though they continued to hope for the return of still others [56.8]). Given the pervasive expression of hope for restoration found throughout the book at all levels, surely these editors did not believe that the divine plan for God's people had come to an end.

Rather, a post-exilic conviction of an ongoing future divine plan impressed itself deeply and broadly on the shape of the book (Berges 1998, Stromberg 2010). The clearest example of this has already been mentioned in Chapter 3 in connection with TI's role in the formation of the book (see pp. 48–53). There it was noted that the entire book of Isaiah has been made to begin and end with the same scenario, in which God judges his people, saving the penitent, but destroying the rebels, thereby producing a righteous remnant who would inherit Jerusalem and the new world accompanying it (1.27-31; 65–66). This strategy will probably have been considered a natural extension of that ongoing divine plan which was the thread holding together all of the earlier events of Israel's history recounted in the book.

4. Conclusion

The point of this whole discussion has been to demonstrate that, while the book of Isaiah is certainly a collection with loose ends, it is also the result of carefully considered literary strategies arising from theological assumptions deeply ingrained in the world view of the book's final editors. These assumptions concern the divine origin of historically dissimilar Isaianic oracles and the unity of divine purpose underlying Israel's tumultuous history. Both assumptions compelled the editors in their work, adding a sense of unity and purpose to a very complex collection. This sense of unity and purpose became textualized in the form of literary strategies intended to generate larger patterns of meaning in the book. Therefore, while some scholars focus exclusively on the reader in seeking holistic understandings of Isaiah, there is more than enough justification to set about this task also with an eye toward the intentions of the Isaianic authors and redactors, being ever mindful that some features of the text may owe their existence more to source than to strategy.

Chapter 6

Approaches to Isaiah's Theology

1. Introduction

By most accounts, Isaiah the prophet was a theologian. He believed in the God of Israel, that this God was active in the life of the people, and that he made himself known to humans. The same can be said of the other authors whose work is now found in the book. Though anonymous, they too had such a faith and expressed it in writing. From its earliest layers to its latest, therefore, the book itself is thoroughly theological. However, it would be wrong to regard the "theological" aspects of Isaiah as separated from history or politics. On the contrary, as we have seen throughout the present study, the prophet and those who followed in his literary footsteps were deeply concerned with the history and politics of Israel and the nations whose own courses impinged on its destiny. They offered full-blooded theological accounts of these terrestrial affairs, and on no less authority than God himself. Most, if not all, of the material in the book claims the status of divine revelation for itself. Hence, the book is permeated with divine speech formulae: "thus says the Lord," "Oracle of the Lord," "Says my God," etc. While all of this will be fairly self-evident even on a casual reading of the book, scholars can mean quite different things when they speak of the "theology of Isaiah." Complicating this phrase are two sets of issues which have been related in different ways.

2. Descriptive or Confessional

The first of these relates to whether one seeks a descriptive approach to Isaiah's theology, or a confessional one. Sailhamer (1995) has given a helpful description of these approaches as they relate to the broader task of defining the theological assertions and assumptions of the Hebrew Bible/Old Testament. "According to the descriptive approach, the task of OT theology is merely to describe the content of what the OT meant to its original readers" (1995: 157). By contrast, "[a]ccording to the confessional approach, the task of OT theology is to define the message of the OT within the context of one's own personal faith. The task of OT Theology is thus not merely to describe the meaning of the text but also to stand under its authority" (1995: 169–170). Whatever the weaknesses of such a definition, it does underscore the very real fact that many people throughout history have read Isaiah from within the context of their own religious tradition, their faith being shaped by Isaiah while also informing their understanding of it. In fact, this mode of reading the book can be traced all the way back to its earliest editors. For, as we have seen, they were the earliest readers of the Isaianic oracles, and they regarded this material as divinely inspired. At the same time, Sailhamer's definition draws attention to the fact that one need not be religious at all to read the words of the book, recognize their theological claim, and describe it. Hence, it will be abundantly clear to anyone reading the throne-room vision of Isaiah 6, that its author (probably Isaiah) wanted to assert that God is "holy," a patently theological assertion (6.3).

While the distinction between descriptive and confessional approaches is therefore a real one, putting things this way is not intended to belie the fact that scholars disagree strongly over the inter-relation of these two approaches. Should a descriptive and non-committed approach be seen as the foundation of all further use of the text? Should it, for example, precede any confessional understanding of the book? What role do assumptions, religious or otherwise, play in our reading of texts? Do they obscure what is there? Do they aid in understanding what is there? Can they do both on different occasions? Is neutrality possible? If so, should we strive for it in our reading? If not, does that free us from seeking it? Can we ever be truly free of our assumptions (be these religious or otherwise) in our perceptions of things, including texts? These questions (and others) are part of an important debate taking place in the philosophy of reading texts, and in the case of reading a religious text like the Bible, the debate is often cast in terms of the relationship between faith and reason. It will come as no surprise that different answers are given to these questions. Not infrequently, biblical scholars will try to solve this issue with a few prescriptive remarks one way or the other, blithely asserting how the problem should be approached. In an effort to avoid such superficiality, I would simply note that the relationship between these approaches is complex, each construal of the issue being infused with a different theory of hermeneutics, to say nothing of epistemology (Barton 2007: 137–186, Boer 2010, Plantinga 2000: 374–421, Seitz 2001b, Stendahl 1962, Vanhoozer 1998). Despite the complexity of this issue, the distinction between descriptive and confessional approaches remains a helpful one in analyzing what scholars set out to do in defining the theology of Isaiah.

If the nature and aims of a descriptive approach seem fairly straight-forward, the same cannot be said of the confessional approach. Contemporary confessional approaches to the Bible, whether Jewish or Christian, emerged from the long history of confessional interpretation of this sacred text, a mode of reading that dominated ancient study of scripture. They are heirs to this history, even in instances where they seek to modify it. Confessional interpretation of the Bible began very early. It is in fact older than the Bible itself. Hence, even before many of its books existed and while others were being written and edited, religious people in ancient Israel were interpreting these texts as sacred scripture (Fishbane 1985, Kugel 1998: 1–41, Seeligmann 1953). We have already seen that this process was at work in the formation of Isaiah itself, but it is also evident in most other books of the OT.

By most accounts, interpretive activity surrounding the Bible greatly intensified in the Second Temple Period (c. 515 B.C.E.–70 C.E.). This intensification probably owed itself to a merging of several different factors. One central factor worth mentioning here is suggested by Kugel — the return from Babylonian exile and the subsequent efforts at restoration.

> Those who went back to Judah doubtless did so for a variety of reasons, but certainly one of them was a straightforward desire to return to the place and the way of life that had been their ancestors' in days gone by. Yet here was a problem. For, while the physical places previously inhabited may have been clear enough, the way of life that had been followed in them was not. One could not interrogate the hills or the trees to find out how one's forebears had acted two or three generations earlier: that information depended on the restored community's collective memory, a memory embodied in (among other things) its library of ancient texts. Thus, the very mode of return — the desire to go back to something that once existed — probably made this community bookish to an abnormal degree (1998: 5).

This is certainly corroborated by the composition of Isaiah, which saw a major stage of development just after the exile, a stage driven by an intense interest in the divine meaning of older Isaianic oracles, oracles which spoke of return and restoration. Thus, the very shape of Isaiah is bound up with the origins of the confessional approach to interpretation. And to the extent that contemporary confessional readings of Isaiah do the same, they are heirs to a theological tradition embedded in the book itself.

Since the contemporary confessional approach derives from this ancient tradition, we can expect to have the most success in describing its overall shape by appealing to its earliest form. While biblical interpretation in the Second Temple Period was certainly diverse, there were also certain shared assumptions among its practitioners. Kugel lists four that he regards as essential to the early readers' way of thinking (2007: 14–16).

> 1. [Ancient interpreters] assumed that the Bible was a fundamentally cryptic text: that is, when it said A, often it might really mean B . . . 2. Interpreters also assumed that the Bible was a book of lessons directed to readers in their own day . . . 3. Interpreters also assumed that the Bible contained no contradictions or mistakes. It is perfectly harmonious, despite its being an anthology . . . 4. Lastly, they believed that the entire Bible is essentially a divinely given text, a book in which God speaks directly or through His prophets.

There was probably some variation in the degree to which any one of these was true for various Jewish and Christian groups of the period. But assuming Kugel is generally right, we may take this as a rough-and-ready guide to the early shape of the confessional approach to scripture.

Of course, these four assumptions have not all fared the same in the subsequent history of confessional interpretation leading up to the present, but there is a broad family resemblance between them and some of the basic tenants of biblical interpretation in much of Judaism and Christianity today. Thus, we may take it that much confessional reading of Isaiah today will have been influenced in one way or another by these assumptions. But, besides this very general point, it is difficult to say more about the confessional approach without focusing too narrowly on one particular construal of it (Hays 2007, Moberly 2009). In its use, "confessional" has proven to be a flexible term, capable of being applied to the readings of people as different as Billy Graham and Rudolph Bultmann. For a sophisticated account of the transformation of the older confessional approaches in the modern period, see Frei (1974).

3. Source-oriented or Discourse-oriented

We have already met with the second set of issues complicating what is meant by "the theology of Isaiah." In Chapter 4, I followed Sternberg's attempt at delineating a major distinction between two types of approaches in biblical studies, that between source-oriented and discourse-oriented analyses.

In the source-oriented approach, "interest focuses on some object behind the text — on a state of affairs or development which operated at the time as a source (material, antecedent, enabling condition) of biblical writing and which biblical writing now reflects in turn" (Sternberg 1985: 15). Applied to the analysis of the theology of Isaiah, this approach might seek, for example, to reconstruct the theology of the historical prophet Isaiah. What did he preach? How was this affected by his political ties to the royal court? How was it conditioned by prophecy as a religious phenomenon in the Ancient Near East more broadly? A source-oriented analysis of Isaiah's theology along these lines will, as a first order of business, strip away all latter additions to the text that do not derive from the prophet himself in order to arrive at what are deemed to be the original sayings of the prophet preserved in the book. It will then seek to place these sayings in their original setting within the ministry of the prophet. Ideally, one will be able to trace every development in the prophet's theological thought, and link these to specific circumstances in the developing history of Israel, thereby locating the origin of each new stage of his thinking. The whole will then be situated within the broader stream of the religious development of ancient Israel. So, rather than focusing on the shape of the book and how that construes the theology of Isaiah, the source-oriented approach grapples with the shape of the history behind the book and how it conditioned the theology of the prophet (cf. Barthel 1997, de Jong 2007).

Discourse-oriented analysis has a different aim. To quote Sternberg again:

> "Discourse-oriented analysis . . . sets out to understand not the realities behind the text but the text itself as a pattern of meaning and effect. What does this piece of language — metaphor, epigram, dialogue, tale, cycle, book — signify in context? What are the rules governing the transaction between storyteller or poet and reader? . . . How does the work hang together? And in general, in what relationship does the part stand to the whole and form to function?" (Sternberg 1985: 15).

Applied to the analysis of the theology of Isaiah, a discourse-oriented approach would interest itself in, for example, how the sayings of the prophet have been taken and woven together into a coherent piece of literature with a strategy, or strategies, aimed at generating larger patterns of meaning. By what literary means is one originally independent oracle connected with another? Why was this done, to what effect? What clues did the authors and editors leave the reader for making sense of the resulting whole? In short, how does the literary context of the book construe the theology of the prophet Isaiah? A discourse-oriented analysis of Isaiah's theology along these lines will begin by looking for meaningful patterns in the text — literary seams connecting one source to another, echoes of one text in another, rewritings of older sources with an eye toward the literary context, purposeful juxtapositions, etc. It will then seek to make sense of these in terms of strategy, how they were to guide the reader through the material, what "spin" they put on it. So, rather than focusing on the shape of the history behind the book and how that conditioned the theology of the prophet, the discourse-oriented approach seeks to explain the shape of the book itself and how it construes the theology of Isaiah (cf. Ackroyd 1978, Childs 2000, Seitz 1993).

Since a discourse-oriented approach assumes that the text is constructed such that a holistic reading of it is possible and desirable, it will often set as its goal to understand the "final form" of the text, as opposed to its putative sources. While such a goal is entirely reasonable, care should be taken not to view the "final form" of Isaiah, and therefore its theology, over simplistically. As we have seen the final form of this book is the product of the editing of sources, so that it contains rough edges which may not all be equally suited to a particular reading of the whole, even if that reading was intended by some later hand (see further Williamson 1995).

The other danger facing an overly simplistic discourse-oriented analysis of Isaiah's theology, in as far as it seeks to read the book's final form, arises from the transmission of the book after it had reached its more or less present shape. After they were put together and "published," biblical books had a long and sometimes theologically productive history of transmission. Since all the manuscripts of these texts had to be copied and recopied as time went on, opportunities arose for changes to enter the text. Some of these changes were unintentional and due to scribal error, but

others seem to have been quite deliberate. Of the latter sort, the text of
Isaiah yields some examples that clearly preserve theological reflection on
the text. As was noted above, nearly all of the people who read the Bible
in antiquity did so confessionally. This was no less true for those charged
with the task of preserving its text: these scribes were also readers and
no doubt followed the hermeneutical conventions of the day (on this in
relation to biblical law see Teeter 2009; in relation to Isaiah see Koenig
1982). I mention this issue in connection with the theology of Isaiah, not
because it has yet to receive attention in the present work (which is true),
but because the theological nature of textual variants is widely under-
appreciated. Two examples should suffice to illustrate the point.

Consider the textual history of Isa. 1.7. Prominent among the well-
known difficulties of its last clause is the ambiguity of the phrase "like an
overthrow of foreigners." Does this mean that the foreigners are the ones
who overthrow, or that they are the ones overthrown? While the use of
"overthrow" elsewhere clearly suggests the latter, the scribe responsible
for the text now in 1QIsa.ᵃ 1.7 (one of the Isaiah scrolls from Qumran)
thought that it referred to the former. This scribe sought to show that it
was the foreigners who would "overthrow" the land of Israel. He did so
by modifying the original text "and a desolation" (*wšmmh*) to read "and
they were appalled over it" (*wšmmw ʿlyh*). As a result, those foreigners
mentioned just prior to the phrase — those who consume the land —
became the subject of the newly created verb "appalled." The foreigners
will be "appalled over" the destruction of the land of Israel. Thus, the
scribe behind the Qumran scroll resolved the ambiguity of the original
text by slightly altering it.

As has been recognized, his clarification of this textual detail took the
form of assimilating Isa. 1.7 to Lev. 26.32: the Leviticus text reads "and
they were appalled over it" (*wšmmw ʿlyh*) like 1QIsa.ᵃ 1.7 (Koenig 1982:
218–221, Skehan 1957: 152). In other words, the scribe responsible for
the change found guidance in the close parallel that would have been
evident between Isaiah and Leviticus *before the expansion*. Compare Isa.
1.7a with Lev. 26.33.

> Your land will become desolate (*ʾrṣkm šmmh*) and your cities (*ʿrykm*) burnt with
> fire. (Isa. 1.7a)

> Your land will become desolate (*ʾrṣkm šmmh*) and your cities (*ʿrykm*) a ruin.
> (Lev. 26.33)

This parallel was present before any alteration to Isa. 1.7, suggesting that
it was the basis for the scribe's work. Hence, the scribe behind 1QIsa.ᵃ
clarified the ambiguity of 'like an overthrow of foreigners' by altering the
text along lines already found in the verse itself, namely, its connection
to the covenant curses of Leviticus 26. In this light, it becomes clear that
the variant reading in 1QIsa.ᵃ 1.7 assimilates to Lev. 26.32. In altering
the text, the scribe amplified the textual echo of Leviticus 26 that he
found in Isa. 1.7. Since Leviticus 26 recounts the curses that were to fall

on the people if they failed to obey the law, the scribe's work emphasizes "exegetically that the fate of Jerusalem is an outworking of the covenant curses in the law" (Williamson 2006: 50).

The change was minor. However, it was part of, and at the same time perpetuated, a deep-seated theological conviction that the judgment prophesied against Israel in Isaiah was that threatened long ago in the contract forged between God and his people at Mount Sinai (cf. Lev. 27.34). This illustrates how confessional readers, the scribes among them, sought to coordinate different books of the Bible which they regarded as inspired (so Kugel's third and fourth assumptions mentioned above). It also shows that an essential ingredient of this was the belief in a single divine history connecting different biblical events, a history within which different biblical books were to be read. Leviticus illuminated Isaiah, because Sinai impacted the land of Israel in Isaiah's day.

A similar variant is found in the Aramaic (Targum) and Greek (Septuagint) translations of Isa. 65.22. Isaiah 65 describes the future that awaited God's people in terms of a new heavens and new earth wherein people would live supernaturally long lives and the animal world would undergo a radical transformation (vv. 17-25). For anyone familiar with the creation narratives of Genesis 1–3, such language will have likely evoked the depiction of paradise in these early chapters. Such was the case for the translators of the Targum and Septuagint, or more likely, for the common text or tradition which they drew on. For, where the original text in 65.22 promises that "the days of my people will be like the days of a tree," both these versions add "like the days of *the tree of life*." This addition clearly derives from the paradise narratives of Genesis where God plants the "tree of life" in the Garden of Eden (2.9), a tree that was capable of giving eternal life to the first couple (3.22). In this case as well, someone responsible for the transmission of Isaiah has altered it in the light of their reading of it, a reading informed by the notion of the divine authority of different books (so that they could be read as, in a sense, one) and the conviction that Isaiah was part of a larger divine history recounted by these books. What was lost in Genesis has been recovered through textual manipulation in Isaiah. The life of the tree once lost would be returned.

While these variants will be regarded by most as secondary changes arising in the stage of transmission, they are no less theological than the "original" composition of the book. As such, they are important witnesses to early confessional readings of Isaiah. But the larger point here is that such variants further complicate the idea of a theology of Isaiah's "final form," showing that this form retained some fluidity even after it was largely complete. Such fluidity need not militate against a satisfying holistic reading of the book; it only need caution us against overly simplistic ideas about its final form. Abundant evidence remains for broader literary strategies woven into the book by its later editors and authors. It is true that such strategies sometimes made their way into biblical books during the stage of "transmission" that we have been talking about, but it is generally agreed that most of the changes that occurred in the text of Isaiah after it reached its present 66-chapter form do not amount to a different edition of the book with its own strategy (Stromberg 2009a, Ulrich 2001: 290). Thus, such changes may complicate the notion of Isaiah's "final form" and any theological analysis of it, but they are not likely to obfuscate the patterns of meaning given the book any more than those loose ends arising from its use of sources. Simply put, the reader needs to be aware that Isaiah owes some of its theological texture to scribal transmission, some to source, and some to strategy.

4. Methodological Permutations

To sum up the main point of what I have said thus far, there can be little debate that Isaiah the prophet had a theology and that the book itself is theological. At the same time, the meaning of "the theology of Isaiah" is complicated by two sets of issues. First, there is the choice between a descriptive and a confessional approach to the book. Scholars can define their aims in terms of a purely descriptive approach uncommitted to the theology of Isaiah, at least while trying to understand it. Or, alternatively, they can seek to understand the theology of that book in terms of their own faith traditions. Second, scholars can seek to understand the theology of a source now incorporated into the book, or they can analyze the theology that arises out of the efforts of Isaiah's editors to give shape to the collection.

These two sets of methodological options can be (and have been) combined in a variety of ways. One can find examples of all possible combinations: Descriptive/Source-oriented, Descriptive/Discourse-oriented, Confessional/Source-oriented, and Confessional/Discourse-oriented. The interrelation of these options can be illustrated as follows.

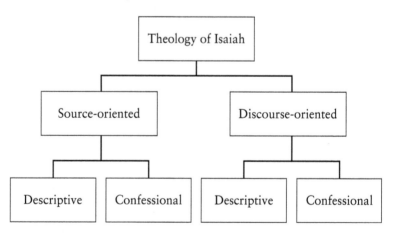

Descriptive/Source-oriented: Here is one example of this approach. Because of DI's exalted language for God and since it was written during the Babylonian exile (a pivotal moment in Israel's history), it has figured prominently in treatments of Israelite monotheism as an historical development. One example is the work of Mark Smith (2001). Smith seeks to examine the emergence of Israelite monotheism in the context of the religions of the surrounding cultures, especially that of Ugarit. Smith's thesis is that the impact of foreign empires on the social structure of Israel led to an elevation in how it spoke about its God.

> Israel's political and social reduction in the world (first because of the rise of empires in the eighth and seventh centuries and then because of the "Exile" in 587–538) further altered its social structure in a manner that had a serious impact on its traditional theology . . . The events leading to the Judean exile of 587 extended Israel's understanding of its deity's mastery of the world even as the nation was being reduced. This shift involves a most crucial change in different Judean presentations of the relationship between the mundane and cosmic levels of reality (or, put differently, between the immanence and transcendence of divinity). As Judah's situation on the mundane level deteriorated in history, the cosmic status of its deity soared in its literature (Smith 2001: 165).

It is this historical process that accounts for the exalted monotheistic rhetoric of DI.

> Before me no god was formed,
>> and after me none shall exist.
> I, I am the Lord;
>> there is no savior besides me. (43.10)

> I am the first and I am the last;
>> besides me there is no other god . . .
> Is there then any God besides me?
>> There is no other rock; I know not one. (44.6, 8)

According to Smith, the language of DI has preserved a distinct moment in Israel's religious development. With the exile came a loss of land and monarchy. Since these defined the older Judean self-understanding, an effort was launched to rework its identity, an identity bound up with its view of God. "Monotheistic claims made sense in a world where political boundaries or institutions no longer offered any middle ground. In its political and social reduction in the world, Israel elevated the terms of its understanding of its deity's mastery of the world." Thus, Smith argues, "monotheism is not a new stage of religion but a new stage of rhetoric in a situation never known prior to the threat of exile." This was not a change in religious policy, but a new "interpretation of religious reality delineating along cosmic lines what was no longer well delineated in the human, political lines" (Smith 2001: 193). This new vision now preserved in DI came to dominate how Israel talked about its God.

Descriptive/Discourse-oriented: This approach was adopted by Brevard Childs in his *Introduction to the Old Testament as Scripture* (1979). The work as a whole has had a major impact on biblical studies, and this is especially true of its treatment of the book of Isaiah. In the preface of his work, Childs seeks to define the aims of his study: "It seeks to describe the form and function of the Hebrew Bible in its role as sacred scripture for Israel. It argues the case that the biblical literature has not been correctly understood or interpreted because its role as religious literature has not been correctly assessed" (1979: 16). Aware that this statement could be interpreted to mean that he is taking a confessional approach, Childs quickly adds that it "is descriptive in nature." He goes on to clarify its aim with particular reference to descriptive and confessional approaches.

> It is not confessional in the sense of consciously assuming tenets of Christian theology, but rather it seeks to describe as objectively as possible the canonical literature of ancient Israel which is the heritage of both Jew and Christian. If at times the description becomes theological in its terminology, it is because the literature itself requires it. The frequent reference to the term 'canonical' is not to suggest that a new exegetical technique is being developed. Rather, the term denotes a context from which the literature is being understood. The subject matter of the Introduction is the received and authoritative writings of ancient Israel which constitute a canon. This analysis is an attempt to hear the biblical text in the terms compatible with the collection and transmission of the literature as scripture (Childs 1979: 16).

One of most important implications of such an approach for Isaiah, as Childs sees it, is to draw attention to the *canonical shape* of the book of Isaiah (1979: 311–338). The faith communities who received the Hebrew Bible did not encounter Isaiah as so many fragments, sources, and redactions. They did not have a "Second-Isaiah" detached from a "First-Isaiah." They received the book as a whole. Childs does not wish to deny the existence of these fragments, sources, and redactions — which he accepts and seeks to integrate into his description. Rather, he wants to draw attention to the ways that the book has been meaningfully shaped into a whole as a result of its use as religious literature.

This, he argues, resulted in the "canonical form of the book of Isaiah," and attention to this illuminates important theological and hermeneutical characteristics of the book (1979: 336–338). One of these is related to DI, about which he argues: "the final form of the literature provided a completely new and non-historical framework for the prophetic message which severed the message from its original historical moorings and rendered it accessible to all future generations" (1979: 337). While this particular argument of his has been criticized because there are historical references in DI (e.g. 45.1), scholars have nevertheless found much descriptive insight in Child's work regarding the shaping and theology of Isaiah. He went on to publish two further studies on Isaiah, one a commentary (Childs 2000) and the other an examination of the history of Isaianic interpretation in the Christian church (Childs 2004). The approaches in each of these works would need a separate description from that given above. Many appraisals of his work have been offered (Barton 1996: 44–56, Seitz 1998: 102–113).

Confessional/Source-oriented: It is not uncommon to find scholars mixing descriptive and confessional approaches in a single study. An example of this is the well-known commentary of Claus Westermann on Isaiah 40–66. While the vast majority of his commentary could rightly be characterized as descriptive, there are instances in which his own religious convictions serve as a theological criterion in interpretation. One such instance comes in his reading of Isa. 66.18-24, the book's concluding vision. This vision depicts a world-wide ingathering of the nations and God's people to the land of Israel where the righteous would participate in perpetual worship, but the wicked would suffer final destruction.

According to Westermann, this vision is composite, consisting of a base layer corrected by a later redaction. The base layer is found in vv. 18-19 and 21. This layer is "governed by the idea of the move out to the Gentiles throughout the world, a missionary move which is destined to reach them all" (1969: 423). The later redaction, which seeks to correct this view, comes in vv. 20, 22-24. This redaction is "governed by the idea of the move towards Zion and Judah, which are to be the scene where the division is made as between eternal adoration and eternal annihilation" (1969: 423). Up to this point, Westermann's analysis seems largely descriptive, even if contested. Then he goes on to remark:

> The fact that vv. 18f. and 21 and vv. 20, 22ff. stand side by side make it terribly clear that in the post-exilic period what people had to say about the way in which God was going to act upon Israel and upon the other nations lost all unanimity and took two different roads. These two passages show both of them, the second being obviously designed to amend the first. *In the light of the New Testament our only course is to agree with the first, the one which proclaims the great missionary move out to the nations. This means, then, that we must be critical of vv. 20, 22ff.* (Westermann 1969: 429, italics mine).

This quote clearly reflects a theological reading of the text wherein preference is given to an earlier layer over and against a later redaction, all under the rubric of Christian confession. As I mentioned above, this sort of explicit confessional approach is not really characteristic of Westermann's commentary. But it does helpfully illustrate an approach to Isaiah's theology that is at once source-oriented and confessional.

Confessional/Discourse-oriented: It would be easy to list a dozen scholars whose work on Isaiah merits this description, but it is probably fair to say that none has argued more eloquently, forcefully, and persistently than has Christopher Seitz for the importance of Isaiah's final form for theological interpretation (1993, 1998, 2001a, 2001b, 2007). Seitz does not deny the composite nature of the text. Rather, he seeks to understand how it has been shaped theologically into what we now have. Not only does he focus on the final form, but he insists upon its central role for understanding how Isaiah is to function theologically within the two-part Christian Bible, an Old and New Testament that together function as authoritative scripture for the church. This focus on the final form differs, of course, from the approach of Westermann above which privileged an earlier layer in the text as being theologically determinative in the light of the New Testament.

5. Conclusions

This chapter has sought to make some sense of what "the theology of Isaiah" could mean in secondary literature on the subject. It could mean the theology of the prophet, as reconstructed when all of the later textual accretions have been removed and what remains has been properly situated in the development of his thinking. Or, alternatively, it could focus on the construal(s) of the prophet's theology in the present shape of the book, by appealing to the literary shaping of it, or by focusing on the role of the reader, or by doing both. These alternatives I have called sourced-oriented versus discourse-oriented approaches. The second issue treated was the choice between a descriptive, non-committed approach to Isaiah's theology and a confessional, committed approach. These two sets of methodological options were seen to be combined in different ways: descriptive/source-oriented, descriptive/discourse-oriented, confessional/source-oriented, and confessional/discourse-oriented.

Chapter 7

Aspects of Isaiah's Theology

Having discussed different approaches to the theology of Isaiah in the previous chapter, I would like here to offer a discourse-oriented analysis of two Isaianic themes that were of special theological significance both to the editors of the book and to its later readers — the destiny of Zion in the prophet's message and, in the light of this, the scope of the royal promises.

I will argue that Isaiah 6 has been edited in such a way as to draw the divine plan revealed to the prophet at his commission into a book-wide strategy involving Isaiah's first chapter as well as its last two, a strategy designed to provide a literary lens through which to view the other oracles in the book. It will be suggested that these other oracles — particularly the royal oracles — were to be read in the light of the future judgment anticipated in the strategy involving ch. 6, a judgment that would purge Israel of the wicked and leave a righteous remnant, a "holy seed."

1. The Prophet Isaiah's Message

If any theological topic can be said to stand at the center of Isaiah it is surely the destiny of Zion at the hands of its God. This theme permeates every level of the book's composition. What would that destiny look like? How would God bring it about? How do the various messages of judgment and salvation figure into it? How does it come across in the message of Isaiah the prophet? It is this last question that will serve to focus our attention on the issue here.

In source-oriented approaches to the question, scholars disagree about how to reconstruct the historical prophet's message as it related to Zion's destiny (Köckert, Becker and Barthel 2003). Did Isaiah preach salvation to his audience, or did he preach judgment? Or, did he preach some combination of both? If Isaiah 6 recounts the prophet's own understanding of his commission, then how can the oracles of salvation attributed to him be reconciled with the message of eventual destruction recounted here

(vv. 9ff.)? If a passage like 1.10-20 can be attributed to the prophet, then how does its exhortation ("learn to do good, seek justice" [v. 17]) fit with the notion that the prophet's ministry would only produce recalcitrance in the people (6.9-10)?

In reconstructing the thought of the historical Isaiah, scholars have proposed different models for relating the messages of salvation and destruction now found in the book which bears his name. Very briefly, there are at least four views presented on the matter. (1) Isaiah preached destruction *and* salvation, the tension between the two being resolved by scholarly appeal to either different audiences, or development in the prophet's thinking. (2) Isaiah exhorted his audience to repentance, announcements of judgment scaring them into this posture, and words of salvation coxing them into it. (3) Isaiah preached inevitable judgment, this being indicated by Isa. 6.9-10 where the message of the prophet only makes the people less responsive, leading to their destruction. The words of salvation only refer to wasted chances at restoration. (4) Isaiah was originally a prophet of hope and salvation, as may be suggested by his close ties to the king and temple. He will have been a sort of advisor to the king, so that it is unlikely that his message would have been only negative. Such are some of the ways scholars have tried to coordinate the oracles of salvation and judgment in the single historical person of Isaiah the prophet.

Whatever the merits of these historical reconstructions, we can see that focusing on how the book itself construes Isaiah's message is a different issue altogether. In a discourse-oriented approach, one is after the *presentation* of the prophet's message, and as the literature construes it, Isaiah emerges as a prophet who preached both salvation and judgment (cf. Ackroyd 1978). Both messages are now found side by side in the book which bears his name (1.1). In this light, we should certainly ask: how does the literary construal deal with the tension between these two messages? How, if at all, are salvation and judgment tied together in the literary logic of the book?

There may be different strategies for dealing with this in the book, but I will focus on the way Isaiah 6 construes it because this chapter promises to illuminate the broader Isaianic tradition for several reasons. To begin with, the prophet is told in 6.9ff. that his message will cause the people to be unresponsive, leading to their destruction. Because critical scholars have traditionally ascribed most of ch. 6 to Isaiah himself, the depiction of the prophet's disturbing task found therein has emerged as a key text in trying to reconcile messages of salvation and judgment in the person of the historical prophet. It is therefore not unreasonable to expect the editors of Isaiah to have wrestled with this same text, had they been inclined to resolve this issue in their own work.

A further reason why ch. 6 should prove to be a productive starting point is that it depicts the commission of the prophet. Here God actually tells Isaiah the scope of the divine plan for his people (vv. 11-13). Since the whole book is subsumed under the prophet's vision (1.1.), what has been said at his commission in ch. 6 will likely have been applied to the rest of the oracles by later readers and editors of the book. This is borne out by allusions to this chapter in nearly every later layer of the book (Clements 1985, Uhlig 2009, Williamson 1994: 46–51). Thus, we noted earlier in our study that DI based its message of hope on the conviction that the judgment announced in Isa. 6.9-10 was now coming to an end (p. 36). Hence, Isa. 41.20 reveals the divine intention in bringing deliverance from exile. God was acting on behalf of his people "so that they *may see and know . . .* that the hand of the Lord has done this." Here one witnesses a reversal of the judgment announced in 6.9-10 where Isaiah was to tell the people "*seeing, see; but do not know*," a condition that would ultimately lead them into exile (v. 12). We saw that Isaiah's commission was also taken up by the even later author of TI, for whom it had a similar meaning (pp. 49–50). While it is certainly possible to argue that the original intent of the commission in ch. 6 was restricted to a limited occasion, these allusions show that it was understood in the book as having a very broad scope, extending to the end of the exile and beyond.

Another reason for thinking ch. 6 may have played a strategic role in construing the oracles of judgment and salvation in the book more broadly comes in the fact that it seems to have been incorporated into a broader literary strategy wherein narratives and headings were interspersed throughout the oracles, most of which are poetic. What is striking about these references is that there was clearly an attempt made to arrange them in chronological order, with 1.1 summarizing the entire scope of the prophet's ministry (6; 7.1–8.4; 14.28; 20; 36–39). Whether this thin layer of narrative was put in place all at once, or is the result of later editing that manipulated earlier sources (which is more likely), the result is clear. The book has been given a chronological backbone that provides narrative accounts of important moments in the ministry of the prophet. But why? What did this contribute to the literary strategy of the book? What was the hermeneutical significance of this move?

Several scholars have argued that these headings and narratives were added to give the oracles historical and biographical context, a sort of narrative context (cf. Ackroyd 1987, Conrad 1991: 34–51, Köckert, Becker and Barthel 2003: 125–126). At first glance, this might seem like a rather mundane conclusion. However, the hermeneutical significance of this move can hardly be overestimated. Without this layer in the book (and a few other slight headings), we would have very little direct evidence in the material itself for attributing the oracles to Isaiah of Jerusalem (cf. Blenkinsopp 2000). And yet, the fact that generations of scholars all the way up to the present have read these oracles in connection with the prophet shows the powerful effect this thin narrative layer wields over its readers. It has functioned as a lens through which the oracular material has been read, a function it no doubt was intended to have.

This is similar to the headings and narratives interspersed throughout the legal material in the Pentateuch. Again the layer is thin, but the effect has been enormous, subsuming vast quantities of law under the figure of Moses. In the light of the deliberate chronological arrangement of this material in Isaiah, we may suppose that it was not only to be a lens through which the oracles were to be read, but more specifically it was to carry the reader along through the book from the Syro-Ephraimite threat (ch. 7), to the Assyrian crisis (chs. 36–38), and up to the threat of Babylonian exile (ch. 39), thereby pushing the reader into chs. 40–66, where this tragic event is everywhere assumed. Saying that these headings and narratives were to impart a chronological reading strategy to the material need not imply that the oracles themselves were subject to a chronological ordering; indeed they were not (see Isa. 1.8-9; p. 22).

The point is that the narratives of Isaiah have been integrated into a broader literary strategy in the book which according to its design has had a powerful effect on how readers have interpreted the oracular material. And therein lays a further reason why the narrative of ch. 6 can be expected to have played a decisive role in the construal of the prophet's message of salvation and judgment reflected in the oracles. As part of this broader strategy, ch. 6 was redeployed as a lens through which to view the surrounding oracular material in the book, a fitting function in the light of its impact on later Isaianic layers which allude to it.

From all of the above, I conclude that whatever is said about the relationship of salvation and judgment in ch. 6 will likely have carried with it implications for the rest of the Isaianic material. With this in mind, we may turn to the chapter itself to see how it construes this central theological problem in the prophet's preaching.

In the first seven verses of this chapter, Isaiah recounts his vision of the Holy One of Israel in such a way as to lead up to his commissioning. The vision so vexes Isaiah that he is compelled to confess "I am a man of unclean lips," an admission anticipating the role he will be given as God's spokesman to the people in v. 9. Confirming the importance of his confession for the narrative structure, immediately one of the seraphim flies over to the prophet and touches his "mouth" with a coal from the altar, thereby removing the "iniquity" of the prophet (vv. 6-8).

With this he is prepared to receive his commission, which follows in the next two verses (vv. 9-10). In Isa. 6.9 God calls out, "whom will I send and who will go for us," and Isaiah answers, "here am I, send me." What God says next has no doubt puzzled readers ever since: "go, say to this people, 'hear but do not understand, see but do not perceive.'" Isaiah was to "make fat" the heart of the people so that they would not hear with their ears or understand with their heart and so turn and be healed (v. 10). Distressed, he asks "how long" ('d mty) this state of stupor would last (v. 11). God answered, "until ('d 'šr) cities are destroyed to the point of being without inhabitant . . . and man is moved away and there is a great forsakenness in the land," until even those who remain in it are destroyed (vv. 11-13). This state of spiritual stupor — effecting a complete devastation of the land — would last until all that remained was a "holy seed." And then, it is implied, it would end. A holy community would survive the judgment to inherit the land.

This then is how ch. 6 construes the relationship between the announcements of salvation and judgment. They constitute an indissoluble whole integrated by a temporal and selective logic. In time, judgment would result in the saving of a few, selected (we may infer) because of their "holiness," a trait echoing the thrice repeated assertion in v. 3 that God is "holy." The temporal dimension of this judgment receives specificity by the description of a destroyed land and, significantly, by the reference to exile in v. 12 — God would "remove" (*rḥq*) the people from the midst of their land. Since it is probable that the relationship between salvation and judgment in ch. 6 will likely have carried with it implications for the rest of the book, surely this reference to exile is significant: it is a theme that now permeates the present shape of the Isaianic collection, as we have seen repeatedly.

Beyond this rather general inference, are there any further signs that this construal of salvation and judgment in the commission of the prophet was to function as a lens through which the book was to be read? It will be recalled from earlier in this study that the last line of ch. 6 is almost certainly a later addition (pp. 18–19; also see Stromberg 2010: 160–174). Nearly all scholars regard this line as the product of a later editor who wanted to identify the "stump" of v. 13 as a purified remnant surviving divine judgment on the people.

> Even if a tenth part remain in it,
>   it will be burned again,
> like a terebinth or an oak
>   whose *stump* remains standing
>   when it is felled.
> The holy seed is its *stump*. (6.13 NRSV)

It is not hard to see the importance of this addition for the theme under discussion. Without "the holy seed is its stump" there would be little to hope for in this passage; it would simply end in judgment.

It will also be recalled from the same discussion that a strong case supports viewing the hand responsible for this addition as that of the author of TI. Without repeating all of the evidence for this here, I would only note the impressive parallel between this addition and the last two chapters of the book, where it is stated in 65.9 that a righteous "seed" would survive divine judgment on the people to inherit the land. Isaiah 6.13 and 65.9 are the only passages in the book employing the term "seed" to describe a righteous remnant emerging from judgment. Thus, it is probable that the editor added the comment about the "holy seed" in 6.13 *in the light of* 65.9 (Stromberg 2010: 160–174).

What was achieved by linking these two chapters in this way? What literary strategy does this produce? The simple answer is that the addition in 6.13 was given as a clue to the reader who would understand the passages in the light of each other. The reader was to see the vision in ch. 65 as a fuller explication of what was already announced to the prophet in ch. 6. Conversely, the reader was to understand the divine plan in ch. 6 as anticipating what is said in ch. 65. Thus, the addition of what amounts to three words in the Hebrew at 6.13 generates a book-wide literary strategy, spanning from the commission of the prophet to the last two chapters of the book.

That this strategy was designed as a lens through which the whole of Isaiah could then be read becomes clear when it is recalled that these final two chapters (65–66) allude to earlier oracles from throughout the book. In doing so, they affirm both the salvation and judgment promised earlier by directing the former to the righteous and the latter to the wicked — all of which was to be fulfilled in a single divine act, still in the future from a post-exilic perspective (Stromberg 2010: 87–141, Sweeney 1997). As with the rest of TI, its last two chapters look back over the book from a post-exilic perspective and conclude that the divine plan for salvation and judgment announced therein still remained on the horizon. Since the divine plan revealed to the prophet in ch. 6 has been drawn into this strategy by the addition of its last line, it too takes on a book-wide scope that is post-exilic in outlook. For this reason also, we may conclude that the construal of the messages of judgment and salvation in ch. 6 was to have been a lens through which the rest of the oracles in the book could be read. In this literary strategy, the divine plan in 6.10-13 for a refining judgment encompassed the whole book, resolving the tension between salvation and judgment by positing a distinction between the righteous and the wicked.

One further detail supports the broad literary scope of the addition in 6.13. This is its connection to the last few verses of the first chapter of the book, vv. 27-31. Both passages describe a purifying judgment with the verb "to burn" (b'r); in 6.13 it is understood this way by the addition. In this sense and within 1–39, b'r occurs only one other time (on 4.4 see Stromberg 2010: 174–183), which may suggest a deliberate connection between 1.27-31 and 6.13. This seems to be supported by other note-worthy parallels between the two passages. For example, in both 6.13 and 1.30 the destruction of the people is compared to a "terebinth" (k' lh), a somewhat rare word that occurs nowhere else in Isaiah. As a result, a fairly strong case emerges suggesting that the passages are related com-positionally, both contributing to the same literary strategy depicting the destiny of Zion in terms of a judgment that separates the righteous from the wicked (Beuken 2004: 83–84, Williamson 1997: 119–128).

With that conclusion in place and to bring the case full circle, we turn to a point mentioned earlier in this study, that 1.27-31 is likely the product of the same hand responsible for chs. 65–66 (pp. 51–53; also see Stromberg 2010: 147–160). If that is correct, then a compositional link between 1.27-31 and the addition in 6.13 offers further support to the claim that the latter was to have a very broad literary *and therefore hermeneutical* scope. The same author has outlined the same scenario of judgment in three key passages in the book, the account of the prophet's commission (ch. 6), the first chapter of the book, and its last two chapters (65–66).

Did this literary construal of Isaiah's vision make itself felt on any other oracles in the book? A strong circumstantial case exists that it did, given the scope of this construal, embracing as it does the first and last chapters of the book and being projected from the pre-exilic ministry of the prophet commissioned (ch. 6) to beyond the post-exilic period (chs. 65–66). Thus, literarily and temporally, the commission is made to span the entire book. It is difficult to see how such a move would have been accomplished in isolation from the other oracles in the book. With this in mind we turn now to the royal oracles in Isaiah.

Isaiah 1.27-31	Isaiah 6.13	Isaiah 65.9
Refining judgment	Refining judgment (b'r)	Refining judgment
(b'r)	Righteous "seed" (zr')	Righteous "seed" (zr')

2. The Scope of the Royal Promises

Space does not permit a full discussion of this here. However, a few suggestions are in order in the light of our preceding discussion. As was true of prophecy in general, the royal oracles of Isaiah were subject to reuse and reinterpretation in various stages of the formation of the book (Clements 1996, Wegner 1992). It is also true that the royal promises were of interest to nearly all levels of the Isaianic tradition (Clements 2003, Stromberg 2009b, Williamson 1998). Since we saw above that the commission in Isaiah 6 has been made a lens through which oracles in the book were to be read (sometimes "reread" when viewed against their original settings), we might expect this to have had some effect on the royal oracles as well (e.g. 9.1-7; 11.1-9). In particular, we may ask whether the royal oracles were reaffirmed by this strategy in the period after the exile, the period to which the key chs. 65–66 owe their composition.

In view of what was said above, the place to begin is obviously with the narrative structure that has been given the book. And here I would note that two of the narratives mentioned deal directly with the royal house and its destiny. Isaiah 7 recounts Ahaz's response to the Syro-Ephraimite crisis, which the narrative frames as a direct threat to the "house of David" (v. 2; also see pp. 86–87). Moreover, the end of the narrative announces to king Ahaz the threat of a future Assyrian invasion which would come on "the house of your ancestor" (v. 17). The other, Isaiah 36–39, narrates Hezekiah's response to the Assyrian crisis, which is also seen as a threat to the house of David (37.35). And it concludes in ch. 39 with an announcement that the temple would be destroyed at the hands of the Babylonians who would also carry away the royal descendants of Hezekiah into exile (39.7). As for the other narratives in the book, we have already mentioned Isaiah 6, which leaves only Isaiah 20. This narrative is closely related to the speech of the Assyrian military official in 36–37, both emphasizing the folly of trust (bṭḥ) in Egypt for deliverance (nṣl) from the Assyrians (note too the use of the "sign" in both). In this light, ch. 20 seems to be connected indirectly with the royal theme of 36–39. Thus, the fate of the royal house of David emerges as a central theme in these narratives.

Since we are interested in how (if at all) these narratives were to relate to the royal oracles in the book, we need to ask whether any connections have been drawn between the two. We have already mentioned two such links in an earlier discussion (pp. 86–93). The first is that between the royal oracle in 9.1-7 and the sign given Hezekiah in 37.30-32. Both conclude with the phrase "the zeal of the Lord of Hosts will accomplish this" (9.7; 37.32). Strengthening the suggestion that this is a deliberate joining of the two, we also saw in our earlier discussion that both have been connected to the overthrow of a foreign yoke. In ch. 37 the phrase is connected to a divine promise that the Assyrian army be repelled "for my sake and for the sake of David my servant" (v. 35). In ch. 9 the removal of the foreign "yoke" is stated in v. 4, a verse that was taken up by 14.25 as the basis for removing the Assyrian "yoke," or indeed that of any nation.

It was precisely in 14.24-27 that the second connection was seen to emerge between the narratives and the royal oracle in 9.1-7. For, while 14.24-27 is grounded in 9.4, it is also connected to 8.9-10, which applies the sign of the Immanuel child mentioned in the narrative of ch. 7 to the mitigation of the Assyrian threat mentioned in 8.7-8. The result was a striking parallel drawn between the child of the royal oracle in 9.1-7 and the child Immanuel, so that they looked as if they were to be identified as one and the same person: a child whose birth signaled the end of the Assyrian yoke. There is therefore clear evidence that the royal narratives of chs. 7 and 36–39 have been interconnected with the royal oracle of 9.1-7 by design.

Having established that there are indeed connections between the narratives and the royal oracle in ch. 9, and that the future of the Davidic house is a central concern of the narratives themselves, the next question to ask is whether these narratives are connected in any way to the strategy involving ch. 6 seen above, a strategy aimed at projecting older oracles into the future of the post-exilic vision of chs. 65–66. To get at this we first need to take a closer look at the strategy formed by the narratives in chs. 7 and 36–39, because whatever is happening in these narratives will have implications for the royal oracle in ch. 9 to which they are connected.

It is now widely recognized that a key element in the strategy involving chs. 7 and 36–39 was their analogical structuring. Analogical structuring of narrative is quite common in the Hebrew Bible, and can involve the presentation of two different events in similar terms, as is the case here (Berman 2004). Sternberg describes the structure and function of such analogies:

> Analogy is an essentially spatial pattern, composed of at least two elements (two characters, events, strands of action, ect.) between which there is at least one point of similarity and one of dissimilarity: the similarity affords the basis for the spatial linkage and confrontation of the analogical elements, whereas the dissimilarity makes for their mutual illumination, qualification, or simply concretization (1985: 365).

That the Ahaz narrative of ch. 7 and the Hezekiah narratives of 36–39 have been made to parallel one another has long been recognized (Ackroyd

1987: 116–119, Conrad 1991: 38–40, Williamson 1994: 191–193). As we have already noted, both narratives reflect a similar situation wherein the Davidic king must respond to an attack by a foreign army. In these narratives there is a clear effort to contrast Ahaz's failure of faith with Hezekiah's piety.

The first verse of each narrative includes a report about the invading army's inevitable advance on Jerusalem. Isaiah 7.1 says the Syro-Ephraimite coalition's attack on Jerusalem was unsuccessful, whereas 36.1 reports that the Assyrians successfully captured Lachish, a neighboring city. Before the two kings are even introduced, then, the narrative is preparing for the contrast: from outward appearances Ahaz has more reason to hope than Hezekiah, casting into deeper relief their opposite reactions. But from the narrative's point of view, outward appearances are irrelevant because each king will be required to trust the word spoken by the prophet, a word of *divine* deliverance. At this Ahaz fails, but Hezekiah succeeds.

After the initial report, someone is immediately sent to the king with a message — Isaiah the prophet to Ahaz, and the Assyrian military official "with a great army" to Hezekiah. Both encounters take place "at the conduit of the upper pool on the highway to the Fuller's Field," a narrative detail quite specific but superfluous, apart from its role in drawing the reader further into the comparison between the two kings and their situations. Further tipping the scales in Ahaz's favor and therefore compounding the guilt of his failure is the hopeful message he is given by the prophet: "do not fear"; the aggressors will not succeed (7.3-9). By contrast, Hezekiah's men and some of the people of the city are made to listen to the elaborate and lengthy threats of the Assyrian military official who, at one point, even goes so far as to tell them they will be forced to consume their own excrement and urine (37). He goes to great lengths to persuade them that the Lord cannot "save Jerusalem from my hand." It is only after Hezekiah hears this and sends for a word from Isaiah the prophet that he is told "do not fear," words long overdue that echo the prophet's immediate though uninvited assurance to Ahaz.

The contrast is further explicated by the next event in each narrative: the king's response and the giving of a "sign" (*'wt*). In 7.10-17, Ahaz is immediately told to ask for a "sign" as confirmation of the prophetic assurance, thereby displaying his faith. He refuses, incurring divine displeasure. Despite his refusal, a sign is given to him that the Syro-Ephraimite coalition would be destroyed by the Assyrians who would then however come against Judah. In 37.9-35, after Hezekiah is told "do not fear" and given a brief word of assurance, he is again confronted with the threatening words of the Assyrians to which he responds in prayer at the temple saying "save us O Lord our God from his hand" (v. 20). Only after all of this does God respond by sending the prophet, who then gives the king a sign that they will be delivered from the Assyrians (vv. 30-32).

All of these parallels feed into the analogical strategy of the narratives. The strategy is not likely one of simple contrast, however. For, both ultimately end with the announcement of a future threat. Ahaz is told the Assyrians would ravage the land (7.17), apparently as a consequence of his lack of faith. Similarly Hezekiah is told that the Babylonians will bring destruction (39.6-7). It may be that this announcement came as a response to Hezekiah's having "rejoiced" over the visit of the Babylonian envoy (v. 2). That the Isaiah editor has at this point altered the original "and he heard" (*wyšmʿ*) of Kings to "and he rejoiced" (*wyśmḥ*) in Isaiah tends to suggest that Hezekiah is being criticized for his overly enthusiastic reception of a foreign power that would later oppress the people (cf. 2 Kgs 20.13). Moreover, he shows them all the treasures in the temple, which Isaiah says they would eventually carry off into exile, along with his royal line. If Hezekiah is being criticized, then in a twist of irony the king whose piety initially contrasted with Ahaz's lack of faith now himself fails; the consequences that we have come to expect by reading the former account are now being applied to the latter, the only difference being that now the Babylonians, not the Assyrians, pose the threat.

It is in any case significant that the reader is carried along by the analogical structure of these narratives to precisely the same existential question facing the house of David. Just as ch. 7 drives the reader into Assyrian crisis, raising the issue of the reliability of the Davidic promise, so ch. 39 pushes the reader into Babylonian crisis, again raising the same issue: will God's commitment to David endure? In its present form, then, this whole structure serves to send the reader searching beyond the announcement of exile in ch. 39 for an answer elsewhere in the book. In the movement of this narrative structure, the existential question about the Davidic house is first raised by ch. 7, and the answer comes in 36–38: the Assyrian threat announced in the former is countered in the latter, thereby reaffirming God's commitment to the royal line and to David (on ch. 7 in this respect, see pp. 86–87). This movement from royal jeopardy in ch. 7 to royal reaffirmation in 36–37 would explain why the royal oracle in 9.1-7, which is connected to the breaking of Assyria "in my land" (14.24-27), is cited in 37.30-32 ("the zeal of the Lord of Hosts will do this" [9.7//37.32]) — 37.30-32 giving the sign that the Assyrian siege would not prevail, that God was committed to defending Jerusalem "on my account and on account of my servant David" (37.35). The Davidic question raised by ch. 7 has been answered in 36–38 through the movement of plot, impelling the reader from the earlier passage to the later. But whence comes the answer to the problem as it is raised again by ch. 39? The narrative strategy again puts the royal promise in jeopardy, again impelling the reader forward in search of an answer.

But should the reader expect to find an answer as he or she presses forward? According to Sternberg, this is a major reason why some biblical narratives were structured analogically — to generate anticipation in the reader that the literary shape of the future will mirror that of the past. Arguing that divine omnipotence figured into the mechanics of biblical narration as a basic assumption, he comments:

> [I]n a God-ordered world, analogical linkage reveals the shape of history past and to come with the same authority as it governs the contours of the plot in fiction. Having traced the rhythm of Genesis, for example, we can predict future

developments which the agents in their shortsightedness can only yearn for or
still hope to block: that Rachel too will be delivered from sterility, say, or that
Joseph will get into trouble but finally prevail (1985: 114).

If analogical narratives generate anticipation in this way, then not only
does the structuring of Isaiah 7 and 36–39 with this technique impel the
reader forward in search for an answer to the question that has been
raised again by ch. 39; it also suggests the reader will find an answer in
the literary future that will correspond with the one given in the literary
past. In other words, because the question raised by ch. 7 was answered
in 36–38, the reader is made to anticipate that when the question is raised
again by ch. 39 it too will be answered in some later part of the book;
and he or she can expect that the answer will mirror that of the past: just
as God honored the Davidic promises in the midst of the Assyrian crisis,
so he will do so again in the midst of Babylonian exile. In the logic of
analogical narrative, the pattern of the past generates expectations for
the pattern of the future. In the "God-ordered world" of the Isaiah narratives, past divine dealings with the Davidic promise are a type of those
in the future — a thought clearly echoed in 14.24-27 which first applies
9.4 of the royal oracle to Assyrian downfall, and then again to that of all
nations, including, by implication of juxtaposition, Babylon, heir to the
role of oppressor (13.1–14.23).

Because analogical narratives generate expectations for the literary
future, we should attach significance to the fact that the announcement
of exile in ch. 39 has been made to introduce chs. 40–66 which seek to
address the existential questions raised by Babylonian destruction, one of
which will have been the future of the Davidic kingdom. For this reason as
well, we may suppose that the aim of the narrative strategy just examined
— which raises existential doubt regarding the Davidic kingdom — was
to send the reader searching for an answer in these later chapters of the
book. However, to know whether or not an answer is given, we, like the
reader, must press on for more definitive evidence.

Such evidence may be found in one feature in particular of the narrative analogy just discussed, the prominent role of the divine "sign" (*'wt*).
How this feature was to guide the reader to an answer later in the book
will, I hope, become clear. But first it is necessary to have a closer look at
these signs in the narratives themselves.

As was noted earlier, the narratives of chs. 7 and 36–39 were not
initially composed for the strategy under examination any more than
ch. 6 was. Rather, like ch. 6 these narratives existed before this strategy
was put in place, and have been adopted and adapted for their present
function in it. Since we are ultimately interested in whether these narratives reflect the same strategy as that found in ch. 6, we should consider
whether they too show any signs of redaction. In ch. 6 was added the
strategically weighty phrase "the holy seed is its stump." Are there com-
parable additions in chs. 7 and 36–39? This is where the role of the sign
in each narrative becomes important. For, scholars have long noted that
the "sign" in both narratives has been manipulated editorially to point

beyond the circumstances of the narratives themselves. It is impossible in the space provided here to list all of the reasons why these signs appear to have been edited. I would simply refer the interested reader to a fuller discussion of this redaction in Stromberg (2010: 205–228) which lists the work of many others on this as well.

In Isaiah 36–39, the evidence for this editing is relatively straightforward if one accepts the majority view that these chapters have been taken over from their original home in 2 Kgs 18.13–20.19, for which they were first composed (pp. 15–16). A simple comparison between Isaiah 36–39 and its counterpart in Kings reveals that the sign in ch. 38 has been reformulated in connection with the addition of Hezekiah's psalm, which is not present in the original. As to why anyone should have been interested in reformulating the sign in ch. 38 will be addressed below.

It is also reasonably clear that the sign in Isa. 7.1-17 has been edited as well, which hardly seems surprising given the close relationship we have already seen between this narrative and that of 36–39. As briefly as possible, it is very widely agreed that the Immanuel sign in 7.14-17 has been edited in order to locate the child in a time after the Assyrians had devastated the surrounding lands of Judah (Duhm 1922: 76, McKane 1967, others are listed in Stromberg 2010: 223 nt. 291). This was accomplished by the secondary insertion of v. 15 between the announcement of the sign of Immanuel's birth in v. 14 and the explanation of the significance of his naming in vv. 16-17, the destruction of the Syro-Ephraimite aggressors and the impending Assyrian threat. Such birth announcements, where the child is named, are common in Hebrew narrative. However, the present instance stands out from all the others in one respect. In every other example where the explanation of the child's name is signaled by the conjunction *ky* ("because"), the explanation follows immediately after the announcement of his birth (so Isa. 8.3-4). In 7.14-17, the comment in v. 15 interrupts this. Thus, v. 15 breaks the pattern found everywhere else, so that it looks secondary to the original form of the sign.

This conclusion is strengthened by the fact that v. 15 appears to be composed by taking a piece of v. 16 and combining it with a piece of v. 22. Apart from slightly different syntax in "to know" (probably necessitated by the joining of these two "pieces"), v. 15 does not actually contain any new words. Hence, v. 15, like v. 16, speaks of a time when the child would "know" how "to reject the bad and choose the good"; and v. 15, like v. 22, says "curds and honey he will eat (*yʾkl*)." That v. 15 should cut and paste together words from its context in this way, and that it should be precisely the element interrupting a pattern found everywhere else in the Hebrew Bible, strongly suggests that it is a secondary insertion into the narrative meant to reformulate the Immanuel sign, a point that is very widely agreed, as we noted.

Why was the Immanuel sign redacted in this way? The cutting and pasting of words from its context suggests that v. 15 was to synthesize different thoughts found there. The purpose of this editorial move is described well by McKane:

the 'butter and honey' of v. 15 derives from v. 22 and consequently the Immanuel sign is projected in v. 15 beyond the Assyrian judgment (vv. 18-20). It is among the remnant in a Canaan from which agriculture and viticulture have been eradicated that Immanuel is located in v. 15 and like them he eats butter and honey (1967: 218).

Thus, the addition in v. 15 was intended to project the sign of v. 14 into a future beyond Assyrian judgment, by placing the child among the remnant described in v. 22. (Incidentally, to the extent that this looks to a time beyond Assyrian oppression it reflects the thought of 8.9-10 whose significance as a universalizing comment on the Immanuel sign we have already noted [pp. 86–93].)

The conclusion that the sign of Immanuel has been edited in this way to point beyond the circumstances of its own narrative and even into a post-Assyrian future dovetails quite well with what was said above concerning the analogical strategy involving this chapter and 36–39, a strategy which moves the reader from one event to the next, ultimately bringing them up to the Babylonian exile. Indeed, in the light of its post-Assyrian perspective, the editorial move underlying v. 15 shows every indication of pointing to the narratives of 36–39, where the Assyrian armies are repelled by the angel of the Lord. That 7.15 should point to these later narratives is hardly an extraordinary conclusion given the close parallel between them and ch. 7. Herein lay the logic of the identification discussed earlier of Immanuel with the child in the royal oracle at 9.1-7. For both appear to be taken up in 37.30-32 — Immanuel, because of the sign given king Hezekiah that he would be part of a post-Assyrian "remnant"; the royal oracle, because of the promise that "the zeal of the Lord of Hosts will do this" (9.7//37.32). Thus, where 37.30-32 looks back to the Immanuel passage, 7.15 looks forward to the sign given Hezekiah of a remnant that will survive Assyrian siege.

We have already seen that chs. 7 and 36–39 are closely bound together through a series of parallels between Ahaz and Hezekiah, so that it hardly seems coincidence that the divine sign in each has been edited. Thus, the editing of both looks very much like it is the work of a single hand, writing into these narratives a single strategy. In this light, if the editing of the sign in ch. 7 was intended to point the reader beyond the immediate circumstances of the narrative, then we may suppose the same intention was at work in the editing of the sign in ch. 38. It is therefore to the editing of the sign in that chapter that we must now turn.

Are there then any indications in the editing of the sign in ch. 38 that it was to point beyond the circumstances of the narrative itself, the period of Assyrian threat? If so, then this should provide us with the clue we have been looking for — the clue that tells whether or not the latter half of the book into which the reader is impelled by ch. 39's announcement of exile actually affirms God's commitment to David, a commitment put into question by that threat of exile, but a commitment whose literary past has generated anticipation of a positive literary future.

There are indeed indications that the editing of the sign in ch. 38, like that in ch. 7, was to point the reader beyond the circumstances of its broader narrative context, in this case chs. 36–39. Understanding why the sign was edited in ch. 38 will require a discussion of another closely related editorial feature of this chapter, the psalm of Hezekiah, which has been inserted into the narrative (it is absent in the original, the Kings parallel). This will require a more extensive discussion than that given to 7.15. After examining this and before moving on, I will try to summarize the argument up to that point, an argument about the royal oracles and their relationship to the narrative strategy of the book.

Developing the earlier argument of Ackroyd, Williamson noted that the addition of Hezekiah's psalm is "one of the few purposeful redactional alterations to the Kings text," and that it "displays an interest in the restored community gathered in worship at the temple" (1994: 210). According to Ackroyd:

> The psalm in Isa. 38 is not simply an appropriately worded psalm of thanksgiving for deliverance in time of distress, here seen as apposite to the recovery of a king. It is a comment on the larger significance of that recovery in the context of the whole work (1974: 345).

Part of that significance, Ackroyd argues, is to be found in the psalm's use of metaphors — such as rescue from the pit — which in other books describe the experience of exile (e.g. Lamentations and Jeremiah). The other part of that significance is to be found in the fact that the climax of the psalm is reached in "the act of praise and worship in which the individual is joined by the community," pointing to a "longed-for restoration of the temple and its worship . . ." (1974: 345). Thus, Hezekiah's death sentence becomes "a type of judgment and exile" and his recovery "a pointer to the possibility of such a restoration for the community" (Ackroyd 1974: 345–346). While one should be careful about pressing every detail of an edited text into a single interpretation, Ackroyd's explanation does capture well the final note of the psalm:

> The Lord will save me, and *we* will play on stringed instruments all the days of *our* life, at the house of the Lord.

Moreover, the psalm was almost certainly added after Jerusalem's downfall at the hands of the Babylonians (it is absent from Kings whose final form is at least exilic). Thus, for this reason and in the light of the psalm's ending, the basic insight of Ackroyd's analysis has rightly won support (Hoffer 1992: 69–84, Konkel 1993: 478–482).

According to Williamson, such an explanation can account in a satisfying way, not only for the inclusion of the psalm, but also, in connection with it, for at least one other significant difference between the Isaiah and Kings accounts of Hezekiah's sickness and recovery. In Isaiah there is a systematic elimination "of some of the details of what the sign was intended to confirm . . . namely that Hezekiah will be 'healed' and that he will go up to the house of the Lord on the third day" (1994: 206). Compare 2 Kgs 20.5-6 with Isa. 38.5, and 2 Kgs 20.8 with Isa. 38.22.

Following Ackroyd, Williamson notes the new emphasis introduced at the end of the psalm, where Hezekiah's "restoration is seen typologically as adumbrating the restoration of the community, characterized by worship in the house of the Lord" (1994: 206–207). He reasons that, since it would have hardly suited this new emphasis to leave a reference "to a single visit at a particular time" as the sign of Hezekiah's restoration (as in Kings), the references were deleted, allowing his healing to be reinterpreted in the light of the psalm. In this way, the insertion of the psalm, with its emphasis on community restoration, offers a neat explanation for the deletion of material in Isaiah 38, material which had as its emphasis the particular healing of one individual at a specific time. Both editorial moves are distinctly Isaianic, being evident vis-à-vis Kings — a fact which further reinforces their inter-relatedness. The insertion of the psalm and the editing of the sign appear to be related.

The redactional connection between the insertion of the psalm and the deletion of this material having to do with the sign finds further support in the new shape and placement given v. 22, the sign Hezekiah requests. Here, Hezekiah's healing and third-day ascent have been deleted, as in v. 5, suggesting the same intention. Moreover, where Hezekiah's return to the temple has been deleted altogether from v. 5, this aspect is retained in v. 22. The result is to separate the sign of vv. 5-8 from the sign of v. 22, so that these are more related in the original Kings version. In the new Isaiah version, the sign of vv. 5-8 focuses exclusively on his healing, and the sign of v. 22 speaks only about his ascent to the temple, an emphasis that van der Kooij notes is well suited to the new stress introduced by the end of the psalm, after which vv. 21-22 have been relocated (2003: 735–736). If the psalm's "climax is reached in . . . the act of praise and worship in which the individual is joined by the community" (Ackroyd 1974: 345), then it is appropriate that v. 22, given its new shape and placement after the psalm, has Hezekiah ask simply: "What is the sign that I will go up to the house of the Lord (*byt yhwh*)?" This question arises naturally from Hezekiah's statement of faith in v. 20: "The Lord will save me, and *we* will play on stringed instruments all the days of *our* life, at the house of the Lord (*byt yhwh*)." Thus, the sign in v. 22 has been shaped to focus solely on, and made to follow, the inserted psalm, which concludes with the concern for the restoration of community worship at the temple.

Therefore, the introduction of the psalm, the deletion of material from vv. 5 and 22, and the positioning of vv. 21-22 after the psalm all appear to be related. All three combine to emphasize a community restoration having worship at the temple as its focus. When compared to its older counterpart in Kings, the sign of Isa. 38.22 now looks forward to the restoration of temple worship spoken of in 38.20 ("*we* will play on stringed instruments all the days of *our* life . . . at the house of the Lord"). This connection with the end of the psalm provides the most obvious motive for the removal and relocation of vv. 21-22 from their original location in Kings. All the weight of the sign now falls on restored worship.

Many scholars have noted that v. 22 ends the account in ch. 38 with a request for a sign which receives no answer in 38–39, the end of the narrative: "What is the sign that I will go up to the house of the Lord?" What function was this unanswered sign request to have served for the reader? Why was the sign edited in this way?

Beuken has offered an attractive suggestion as to how Hezekiah's open-ended question was to function in the text.

> Since the request for a sign remains unanswered, the narrative remains open-ended, allowing it to function well in the perspective of the exile with its hoped for return to and ascent to a refurbished temple (2000: 386).

Such a function fits well with what was already seen to be the case in the editorial work outlined above, with Hezekiah's restoration now adumbrating that of the community. In support of Beuken's view, we can cite two additional points.

First, it is significant in the light of Beuken's emphasis on exile that this narrative ends with an announcement of the coming Babylonian exile (39.6-8). His suggestion that the open-ended question functioned well in the exile dovetails nicely with the widely held view that the Hezekiah narrative has been made to serve as an introduction to the remainder of the book. Everything that follows ch. 39 has as its central purpose the addressing of the existential problem raised by exile. Thus, the open-ended question further impels the reader into these chapters for an answer. It is to be noted in connection with this that Hezekiah's question dealt with precisely the restoration of, not just the community to temple worship, but also the royal line: so the reference to Hezekiah's "sons" in v. 19 who are part of the "we" of v. 20 (Williamson 1996: 52). Thus, for the redactor, Hezekiah's question was likely laden with significance for the Davidic promises.

The second point supporting Beuken's interpretation is a pattern in the book noted by Melugin regarding the use of the sign:

> The sign is crucial in the Syro-Ephraimite war (7,11.14; 8,18); it appears thrice in the narratives about the latter part of Hezekiah's reign, a group of narratives which are pivotal in the collection (37,30; 38,7.22); the carefully arranged kerygmatic unity composed of chapters 40-55 ends with a reference to a sign (55,13); at the end of Isaiah (66,19) the redactor has chosen to speak of a sign (1976: 178).

The editor of 38.22 was clearly interested in recasting the sign Hezekiah requested so that it would emphasize his desire for a return to the temple — a return probably adumbrating the restoration of the community after exile. It is therefore significant that Deutero-Isaiah and Trito-Isaiah each end with a "sign" (ʾwt) connected both to a return from exile and to a restoration of temple worship (55.13; 66.19). In all of 40–66, the term "sign" occurs only otherwise at 44.25, and there it is found in an entirely different connection.

In 66.19-21, it is said that God will place a "sign" (ʾwt) that initiates a return back to "my holy mountain," a phrase referring to the temple in 56.7 ("my house of prayer"). Isaiah 66.20 compares the returning

Israelites to gifts brought to "the house of the Lord," a phrase not used since the Hezekiah narratives and only found one other time in the book. Of those who return some will be taken as "Levitical priests" (v. 21), clearly a reference to those who would serve at the temple.

In 55.13, it is said that the return from exile (v. 12) would be "for the Lord a *name* and an *eternal* sign (*'wt*) *that will not be cut off.*" This is taken up by 56.5 which transforms it into a promise of access to the temple for the obedient eunuch: "In my house and in my walls . . . I will give him an *eternal name that will not be cut off*" (cf. Beuken 1986: 50–52, Davies 1989: 118). In this way, the sign of 55.13 that signaled return now also signals restoration to temple worship. Isaiah 56.1-8 further develops the theme of a promised place in temple worship, and ends in v. 8 with a hope of return parallel to 66.18 (Koenen 1990: 29–31, Tiemeyer 2006: 70–71).

Thus, in both passages the sign is connected with a return from exile and restoration of the community to temple worship. That this is so, and that these signs occur at the strategically significant positions of the end of both DI and TI — both sections that assume the exile, like the end of the Hezekiah narrative — supports Beuken's suggestion that Hezekiah's open-ended question was to serve in an exilic context, "with its hoped for return to and ascent to a refurbished temple." It also strongly suggests that the shaping of v. 22 was undertaken with an eye toward these later texts, in accordance with Melugin's observation. If so, v. 22's editor almost certainly intended the open-endedness of the question to point forward to (and ultimately beyond) the exilic context of the latter half of the book where the restoration of that temple is assured in connection with the divine "sign."

Just like the editing of the Immanuel sign in 7.15 then, the editing of the Hezekiah sign in 38.22 points the reader beyond the circumstances of the narrative itself. Thus, through an editorial redeployment of the sign in each, the narrative strategy of Isaiah shows itself once again to be directing the reader's attention to the latter half of the book, chs. 40–66. And because the editing of 38.22 emphasizes restoration of community worship at the temple, the significance of which is drawn out by the announcement of exile in ch. 39, the reader impelled forward was probably supposed to find the answer to Hezekiah's question ("what is the sign?") in that latter half of the book where "sign" occurs twice more, signifying in each instance the return from exile and the access of temple (55.13; 66.19).

There is then a book-wide strategy wherein the narratives dealing with the royal house employ prophetic signs to carry the reader from Assyrian oppression to Babylonian oppression. How does this "sign" strategy answer the existential doubt raised about the Davidic promise by the announcement of Babylonian exile in ch. 39? We have already seen that the same doubt was raised by ch. 7 and answered in 36–38, that the Assyrian threat announced in the former was quelled in the latter. Jerusalem and its king were delivered, even if surrounding cities were not. Moreover, we have now seen that the editing of the sign of Immanuel reflects this movement from Davidic jeopardy to Davidic reaffirmation.

Through the editing evident in 7.15, the "sign" Immanuel became part of a band of survivors that would remain after Assyrian attack — precisely the thought reflected in the sign given Hezekiah, a sign that he would be part of a remnant that would survive Assyrian siege (37.30-32). Thus, through the editing evident in 7.15, both signs become prophecies offering the same assurance, only the former sign was announced to Ahaz, and the latter to Hezekiah. Both are connected to the royal oracle in 9.1-7 — 37.32 through a citation of 9.4, and 7.14 on account of 8.9-10's relationship to 14.24-27 which cites 9.4. With both signs being grounded in the royal oracle in this way, their fulfillment with the repelling of the Assyrians and the sparing of a remnant reaffirms the Davidic promises.

But what of the new threat announced in ch. 39, Babylonian exile? Does the editing of the sign in ch. 38 with a view toward 55.13 and 66.19 seek to provide a similar answer? If in analogical narratives like these the pattern of the past generates expectation for the pattern of the future, then we should expect that the editing will do precisely this. The signs in the latter half of the book, to which Hezekiah's unanswered sign-request directs us, should lead to the answer we will have come to expect. It is to these signs therefore that we, like the reader, must now turn our attention.

To begin with, it will be recalled from above that both of these signs are now connected to a return from exile and restoration of the community to temple worship (66.19; and 55.13 in connection with 56.1-8). The promise of return provides a general assurance of renewal after exile. The divine commitment to restore community to temple worship could very well be a reaffirmation of the Davidic promise, since the promise of a temple was part of that covenant (cf. 2 Sam. 7.13). And in this connection it is certainly noteworthy that the sign in 55.13 concludes a chapter which offered the exiles a renewal of that promise in v. 3: "the eternal covenant, the sure mercies to David" (Williamson 1978). What this offer was to entail is a matter of some debate; TI understands it in connection with the Davidic promise of a temple (Stromberg 2009b). Whatever else it intends of offer, it is clear that this passage reaffirms the ongoing divine commitment to the Davidic promise in the context of exile. It is therefore significant that this whole chapter concludes in v. 13 with a reference to the "sign." If the two strategic uses of "sign" in 40–66 both echo the Davidic covenant (because of their connection to the temple), we may suppose that here the reader is being given a positive answer to the existential question raised in ch. 39 about the Davidic promises. The divine commitment to David would endure the exile.

However, we need to consider more carefully the last two chapters of the book. For it is there that the book-wide strategy employing the "sign" ultimately lands the reader (66.19). As with ch. 6, the reader is again directed by the narrative frame to chs. 65–66. With that in mind, we may now turn our attention to the royal oracles themselves to see what effect (if any) this was to have upon them. Are there any indications in these last two chapters that this strategy concerned itself with addressing the existential question raised by the announcement of exile in ch. 39: would the Davidic promises endure the exile? We have already seen that a positive answer is suggested by the sign in 55.13 in as far as this was to be connected to temple restoration and the "sure mercies of David" offered the exiles in 55.3. Can the same be said of the last two chapters of the book, the place where the reader is ultimately led by the sign and the analogical strategy of which it is a part? Do these two chapters show any indication that the Davidic promise of the royal oracles would figure into the post-exilic vision painted there?

In our discussion of ch. 6, we noted wide agreement that chs. 65–66 allude to material from throughout the book. It is also true that these last two chapters of the book constitute a single vision (Stromberg 2010: 42–67). Because they allude to earlier passages in the book, we should consider whether any of these allusions are relevant to the question we have been asking. Indeed, two allusions are relevant.

The first of these received a lengthy discussion earlier in this study (pp. 67–70). It was seen there that 65.25 alludes to the royal oracle in ch. 11 in an effort to evoke for the later reader the royal promises found in the earlier passage. Isaiah 65.25 cites the peaceful vision of 11.6-9 which, because it is causally dependent on the reign of the king in 11.1-5, would cause the reader to regard the full vision of 11.1-9 as remaining firmly on the horizon of the post-exilic future described at the end of the book. By most accounts, the citation of the royal oracle in ch. 65 implies that at least some aspect of it is being reaffirmed by this later perspective. Thus, it would seem that as the narrative strategy of the book has led the reader to these final chapters, he or she is now being reminded of what they read along the way. Given that the last two chapters of the book are post-exilic, this citation seems to provide solid evidence that the royal promise was being reaffirmed after Babylonian exile, a thought anticipated by the redaction of ch. 11 itself (on 11.10, see Stromberg 2010: 183–205). Moreover, because we began our examination of the scope of the royal oracles by asking how the narrative strategy of the book might relate to them, it is significant that that strategy has led us here, to 65–66, where one of those royal oracles is being cited in reaffirmation of the Davidic promise.

The second relevant allusion in these two chapters is closely related to this. Chapters 65–66 envision a moral division among the people "Jacob and Judah" such that the wicked are destroyed and the righteous — the "seed" that survives judgment — inherit the land (65.9). It is this "seed" that would enjoy the new heavens and earth whose description is concluded with the citation of the royal oracle in ch. 11 (i.e. 65.25). The second relevant allusion is of a piece with this scenario and, significantly, the allusion is to the sign given Hezekiah in 37.30-32, a sign that was tied to Immanuel, that cites the royal oracle 9.1-7, and that speaks of a remnant which would survive catastrophe. Facing the threat of Assyrian annihilation, Hezekiah was given a sign as assurance of the coming deliverance. He was told:

> This is the sign for you . . . in the third year sow and reap, and *plant vineyards and eat their fruit* (wnṭ῾w krmym w᾽klw prym). (37.30)

In this sign, the people's eventual recovery of agriculture and viticulture was to signify the future re-emergence of a remnant from Jerusalem (v. 32). Just as they would eventually be able to enjoy the "fruit" (*pry*) of their own vineyards, so "the remaining escapees of the house of Judah would take root downward and bear fruit (*pry*) upward" (v. 31). A remnant would survive and flourish.

Precisely this passage is cited to describe the conditions of the new heavens and earth that the remnant in ch. 65 would enjoy (Stromberg 2010: 97–101, Sweeney 1997: 468). Isaiah 65.21 takes the sign of deliverance as a promise for the remnant in the new Jerusalem. It is said of that remnant that,

They will *plant vineyards and eat their fruit* (*wnṭʿw krmym wʾklw prym*). (65.21)

With this allusion to the sign given Hezekiah in ch. 37 the analogical logic discussed earlier wherein the pattern of the literary past generates expectations for what is to happen in the literary future emerges into full view. That past sign of ch. 37, based on the royal promise of ch. 9 and echoing the Immanuel remnant of ch. 7, becomes the basis for the remnant of 65–66, a remnant that would enjoy the royal promises of ch. 11. Not only do these allusions reaffirm the Davidic promises after exile, they also further draw the royal oracles of chs. 9 and 11 into a book-wide narrative strategy thematizing the literary future through the use of the divine sign (see the following chart for a partial summary of this [the arrows indicate the unfolding of literary strategy, not the direction of literary dependence]).

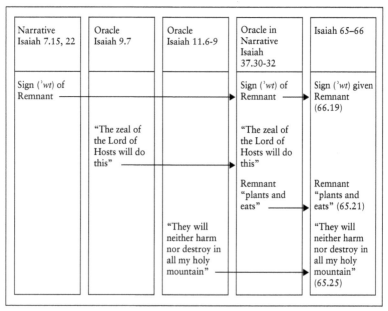

Narrative Isaiah 7.15, 22	Oracle Isaiah 9.7	Oracle Isaiah 11.6-9	Oracle in Narrative Isaiah 37.30-32	Isaiah 65–66
Sign (*ʾwt*) of Remnant ———→			Sign (*ʾwt*) of Remnant ———→	Sign (*ʾwt*) given Remnant (66.19)
	"The zeal of the Lord of Hosts will do this" ———		"The zeal of the Lord of Hosts will do this"	
			Remnant "plants and eats" ———	Remnant "plants and eats" (65.21)
		"They will neither harm nor destroy in all my holy mountain" ———		"They will neither harm nor destroy in all my holy mountain" (65.25)

We may conclude our discussion of the scope of the royal oracles by bringing all of this back to the passage which originally framed the question, ch. 6, the commission of the prophet Isaiah. Earlier we concluded that this chapter had been edited in such a way as to draw the divine plan revealed to the prophet at his commission into a book-wide strategy involving Isaiah's first chapter as well as its last two, a strategy designed to provide a literary lens through which to view the other oracles in the book. These oracles were to be read in the light of the future judgment anticipated in the strategy, a judgment that would purge Israel of the wicked and leave a righteous remnant, or, to put it in the words of the addition at 6.13, a "holy seed." In approaching the question of the scope of the royal oracles, we then wondered whether these might show signs of having been taken up into this book-wide strategy, which concludes in the last two chapters of the book. In the light of the above discussion, we may conclude that they do: the royal oracles have also been taken up by the narrative strategy of the book that reaches its literary end point in the book's conclusion.

Does this mean that the remnant to which Immanuel belonged in ch. 7 was understood as that eschatological remnant in the preceding chapter, the "holy seed" in 6.13? It seems likely when seen in terms of this literary strategy. The editing of the sign in ch. 7 is initially echoed in ch. 37, which is then seen as a prophecy of that righteous "seed" from Jacob in 65.9, the same seed announced in 6.13 (see the chart below). The remnant, to which Immanuel belonged (7.15, 22), was an eschatological one, a conclusion Duhm reached long ago (1922: 76).

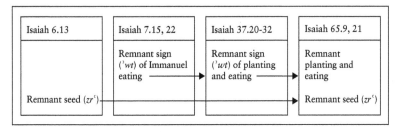

Isaiah 6.13	Isaiah 7.15, 22	Isaiah 37.20-32	Isaiah 65.9, 21
	Remnant sign (*'wt*) of Immanuel eating ⟶	Remnant sign (*'wt*) of planting and eating ⟶	Remnant planting and eating
Remnant seed (*zr'*)		⟶	Remnant seed (*zr'*)

Further Reading

Chapter 1: The Formation of First-Isaiah

The following works may be mentioned as helpful starting points for the topic of this chapter. For an accessible introduction to the formation of PI, see Barton (1995). A useful survey of research on this topic (now translated into English) is that of Wildberger (2002: 513–559). Wildberger's discussion can be updated by reference to Williamson (2009).

Chapter 2: Second-Isaiah and the Book

The following works may be mentioned as helpful starting points for the topic of this chapter. For discussions of the formation of DI, compare the approach of Melugin (1976) with that of Albertz (2004: 376–434). The reader will find a consideration of DI in relation to the formation of the book in Williamson (1994).

Chapter 3: Third-Isaiah and the Book

The following works may be mentioned as helpful starting points for the topic of this chapter. For an introduction to the formation of TI, see Smith (1995) and Emmerson (1992). The reader will find a recent discussion in English of TI's role in the formation of the book (with much further literature on the topic) in Stromberg (2010).

Chapter 4: Literary Approaches to Isaiah

The following works may be mentioned as helpful starting points for the topic of this chapter. For the idea of a literary approach to the Bible, see Sternberg (1985). For literary approaches to Isaiah see Conrad (1991) and Darr (1994).

Chapter 5: Reading Isaiah Holistically

For works attempting a holistic reading of the book from the point of view of "reader-response" criticism, see Conrad (1991) and Darr (1994). For studies seeking to ground a holistic reading in the redaction of Isaiah, see Clements (1985) and Seitz (1990). For some cautionary remarks regarding reading Isaiah as a "unity," see Barton (1998) and Carr (1993).

Chapter 6: Approaches to Isaiah's Theology

In addition to the works mentioned in ch. 6, compare the following different approaches to Isaiah's theology: Heschel (1962: 61–97, 145–158), Rendtorff (2005: 167–200), and von Rad (1965: 147–175, 238–262).

Bibliography

Ackroyd, P. R. (1974), "An Interpretation of the Babylonian Exile: A Study of 2 Kings 20, Isaiah 38-39," *SJT* 27, 329–352.

——(1978), "Isaiah i-xii: Presentation of a Prophet," *Congress Volume: Göttingen 1977*, VTSup 29 (Leiden: Brill).

——(1987), "Isaiah 36-39: Structure and Function," *Studies in the Religious Tradition of the Old Testament* (London: SCM), 105–120.

Albertz, R. (2004), *Israel in Exile: The History and Literature of the Sixth Century* B.C.E., SBLStBL 3 (Leiden and Boston, MA: Brill).

Alter, R. (1981), *The Art of Biblical Narrative* (New York: Basic Books).

——(1985), *The Art of Biblical Poetry* (New York: Basic Books).

Barth, H. (1977), *Die Jesaja-Worte in der Josiazeit*, WMANT 48 (Neukirchen-Vluyn: Neukirchener Verlag).

Barthel, J. (1997), *Prophetenwort und Geschichte. Die Jesajaüberlieferung in Jes 6-8 und 28-31*, FAT 19 (Tübingen: Mohr Siebeck).

Barton, J. (1992), "Redaction Criticism (OT)," in D. N. Freedman, *et al.* (eds.), *The Anchor Bible Dictionary* 5 (New York: Doubleday), 644–647.

——(1995), *Isaiah 1-39*, OTG (Sheffield: Sheffield Academic Press).

——(1996), *Reading the Old Testament: Method in Biblical Study* (Louisville, KY: Westminster John Knox).

——(1998), "What is a Book? Modern Exegesis and the Literary Conventions of Ancient Israel," in J. C. de Moor (ed.), *Intertextuality in Ugarit and Israel*, OTS 40 (Leiden: Brill), 1–14.

——(2007), *The Nature of Biblical Criticism* (Louisville: Westminster).

Becker, U. (1997), *Jesaja — Von der Botschaft zum Buch*, FRLANT 178 (Göttingen: Vandenhoeck & Ruprecht).

Berges, U. (1998), *Das Buch Jesaja: Komposition und Endgestalt*, HBS 16 (Freiburg: Herder).

Berlin, A. (1983), *Poetics and Interpretation of Biblical Narrative* (Sheffield: The Almond Press).

——(1992), "Parallelism," in D. N. Freedman, *et al.* (eds.), *The Anchor Bible Dictionary* 5 (New York: Doubleday), 155–162.

Berman, J. A. (2004), *Narrative Analogy in the Hebrew Bible. Battle Stories and Their Equivalent Non-battle Narratives*, VTSup 103 (Leiden: Brill).

Beuken, W. A. M. (1986), "Isa. 56.9-57.13 — An Example of the Isaianic Legacy of Trito-Isaiah," in J. W. van Henten, H. J. De Jonge, P. T. Van Rooden, and J. W. Wesselius (eds.), *Tradition and Re-Interpretation in Jewish and Early Christian Literature: Essays in Honor of Jürgen C.H. Lebram* (Leiden: Brill), 48–64.

——(2000), *Isaiah 28-39*, trans. B. Doyle, HCOT (Leuven: Peeters).

——(2004), "The Manifestation of Yahweh and the Commission of Isaiah: Isaiah 6 Read against the Background of Isaiah 1," *CTJ* 39, 72–87.

Blenkinsopp, J. (2000), "The Prophetic Biography of Isaiah," in E. Blum (ed.), *Mincha. Festgabe für Rolf Rendtorff zum 75. Geburtstag* (Neukirchen-Vluyn: Neukirchener Verlag), 13–26.

——(2003), *Isaiah 56-66*, AB 19B (New York: Doubleday).

Boer, R. (ed.), (2010), *Secularism and Biblical Studies* (London: Equinox).

Carr, D. (1993), "Reaching for Unity in Isaiah," *JSOT* 7, 61–80.

Chapman, S. B. (2000), *The Law and the Prophets: A Study in Old Testament Canon Formation*, FAT 27 (Tübingen: Mohr Siebeck).

Childs, B. (1979), *Introduction to the Old Testament as Scripture* (Philadelphia: Fortress Press).

——(2000), *Isaiah*, OTL (Louisville, KY: Westminster).

——(2004), *The Struggle to Understand Isaiah as Christian Scripture* (Grand Rapids, MI: Eerdmans).

Clements, R. E. (1980), *Isaiah 1-39*, NCBC (Grand Rapids, MI: Eerdmans).

——(1985), "Beyond Tradition History: Deutero-Isaianic Development of First Isaiah's Themes," *JSOT* 31, 95–113.

——(1989), "Isaiah 14,22-27: A Central Passage Reconsidered," in J. Vermeylen (ed.), *The Book of Isaiah*, BETL 81 (Leuven: Leuven University Press and Peeters), 253–262.

——(1996), "The Immanuel Prophecy of Isaiah 7.10-17 and its Messianic Interpretation," in R. E. Clements (ed.), *Old Testament Prophecy: From Oracles to Canon* (Louisville, KY: Westminster John Knox Press), 65–77.

——(2003), "The Davidic Covenant in the Isaiah Tradition," in A. D. H. Mayes and R. B. Salters (eds.), *Covenant as Context: Essays in Honour of E. W. Nicholson* (Oxford: Oxford University Press), 39–69.

Clifford, R. J. (1980), "The Function of Idol Passages in Second Isaiah," *CBQ* 42, 450–464.

Collins, J. J. (1992), "Early Jewish Apocalypticism," in D. N. Freedman, *et al.* (eds.), *The Anchor Bible Dictionary* 1 (New York: Doubleday), 282–288.

Conrad, E. W. (1991), *Reading Isaiah*, OBT (Minneapolis: Fortress).

Darr, K. P. (1994), *Isaiah's Vision and the Family of God* (Louisville, KY: Westminster John Knox).

Davies, G. I. (1989), "The Destiny of the Nations in the Book of Isaiah," in J. Vermeylen (ed.), *The Book of Isaiah*, BETL 81 (Leuven: Peeters/Leuven University Press), 93–120.

de Jong, M. (2007), *Isaiah among the Ancient Near Eastern Prophets: A Comparative Study of the Earliest Stages of the Isaiah Tradition and the Neo-Assyrian Prophecies*, VTSup 117 (Leiden: Brill).

Dever, W. G. (2007), "Archaeology and the Social World of Isaiah," in R. B. Coote and N. K. Gottwald (eds.), *To Break Every Yoke: Essays in Honor of Marvin L. Chaney* (Sheffield: Sheffield Phoenix), 82–96.

Driver, S. R. (1920), *An Introduction to the Literature of the Old Testament* (New York: Charles Scribner's Sons).

Duhm, B. (1892), *Das Buch Jesaia*, HKAT (Göttingen: Vandenhoeck & Ruprecht).

——(1922), *Das Buch Jesaia*, 4th ed., HKAT (Göttingen: Vandenhoeck & Ruprecht).

Elliger, K. (1928), *Die Einheit Tritojesaia*, BWANT 45 (Stuttgart: Kohlhammer).

——(1933), *Deuterojesaja in seinem Verhältnis zum Tritojesaja*, BWANT 63 (Stuttgart: W. Kohlhammer).

Emerton, J. A. (1982), "The Translation and Interpretation of Isaiah vi. 13," in J. A. Emerton and S. C. Reif (eds.), *Interpreting the Hebrew Bible: Essays in Honour of E.I.J. Rosenthal* (Cambridge: Cambridge University Press), 85–118.

——(1993), "The Historical Background of Isaiah 1:4-9," in S. Ahituv and B. A. Levine (eds.), *Avraham Malamat Volume*, EI 24 (Jerusalem, 34–40).

Emmerson, G. I. (1992), *Isaiah 56-66*, OTG (Sheffield: JSOT Press).

Erlandsson, S. (1970), *The Burden of Babylon. A Study of Isaiah 13:2-14:23*, ConB, OT Ser. 4 (Lund: CWK Gleerup).

Exum, J. C. (1979), "Isaiah 28-32: A Literary Approach," *SBL 1979 Seminar Papers* 2 (Missoula: Scholars Press), 123–151.

Fishbane, M. (1981), "Recent Work on Biblical Narrative," *Prooftexts* 1, 99–104.

——(1985), *Biblical Interpretation in Ancient Israel* (Oxford: Clarendon Press).

Fohrer, G. (1962), "Jesaja 1 als Zusammenfassung der Verkündigung Jesajas," *ZAW* 74, 251–268.

Frei, H. (1974), *The Eclipse of Biblical Narrative* (New Haven, CT: Yale University Press).

Gonçalves, F. J. (1999), "2 Rois 18,13-20,19 par. Isaïe 36-39. Encore une fois, lequel des deux livres fut le premier?" in J.-M. Auwers and A. Wénin (eds.), *Lectures et relectures de la bible: Festschrift P.-M. Bogaert*, BETL 144 (Leuven: Leuven University Press), 27–55.

Gosse, B. (1996), "Isaiah 8.23b and the Three Great Parts of the Book of Isaiah," *JSOT* 57–62.

Gressmann, H. (1914), "Die literarische Analyse Deuterojesajas," *ZAW* 34, 254–297.

Gunn, D. M. (2000), "Hebrew Narrative," in A. D. H. Mayes (ed.), *Text in Context: Essays by Members of the Society for Old Testament Study* (Oxford: Oxford University Press), 223–252.

Hagelia, H. (2006), "The Holy Road as a Bridge: The Role of Chapter 35 in the Book of Isaiah," *SJOT* 20, 38–57.

Haran, M. (1963), "The Literary Structure and Chronological Framework of the Prophecies of Is. XL-LXVI," *Congress Volume: Bonn 1962*, VTSup 9 (Leiden: Brill), 127–155.

Hays, C. B. (2008), "Echoes of the Ancient Near East? Intertextuality and the Comparative Study of the Old Testament," in J. R. Wagner, C. K. Rowe and A. K. Grieb (eds.), *The Word Leaps the Gap: Essays on Scripture and Theology in Honor of Richard B. Hays* (Grand Rapids, MI: Eerdmans), 20–43.

Hays, R. B. (2005), *The Conversion of the Imagination: Paul as Interpreter of Israel's Scripture* (Grand Rapids, MI: Eerdmans).

——(2007), "Reading the Bible with Eyes of Faith: The Practice of Theological Exegesis," *JTI* 1, 5–21.

Heschel, A. J. (1962), *The Prophets* 1 (New York: Harper & Row).

Hibbard, J. (2006), *Intertextuality in Isaiah 24-27: The Reuse and Evocation of Earlier Texts and Traditions*, FAT 2nd Series 16 (Tübingen: Mohr Siebeck).

Hoffer, V. (1992), "An Exegesis of Isaiah 38.21," *JSOT* 56, 69–84.

Höffken, P. (2004), *Jesaja: Der Stand der theologischen Diskussion* (Darmstadt: Wissenschaftliche Buchgesellschaft).

Hutton, J. (2007), "Isaiah 51:9-11 and the Rhetorical Appropriation and Subversion of Hostile Theologies," *JBL* 126, 271–303.

Kaiser, O. (1974), *Isaiah 13-39*, trans. R. A. Wilson, OTL (Philadelphia: Westminster).

Köckert, M., U. Becker, and J. Barthel. (2003), "Das Problem des historischen Jesaja," in I. Fischer, K. Schmid, and H. G. M. Williamson (eds.), *Prophetie in Israel*, Altes Testament und Moderne 11 (Münster: LIT Verlag), 105–136.

Koenen, K. (1990), *Ethik und Eschatologie in Tritojesajabuch*, WMANT 62 (Neukirchen-Vluyn: Neukirchen Verlag).

Koenig, J. (1982), *L'Herméneutique analogique du Judaïsme antique d'après les témoins textuels d'Isaïe*, VTSup 33 (Leiden: Brill).

Konkel, A. H. (1993), "The Sources of the Story of Hezekiah in the Book of Isaiah," *VT* 43, 462–482.

Kooij, A. v. d. (2003), "Textual Criticism of the Hebrew Bible: Its Aims and Method," in S. M. Paul, *et al.* (eds.), *Emanuel. Studies in Hebrew Bible, Septuagint, and Dead Sea Scrolls in Honor of Emanuel Tov*, VTSup 94 (Leiden: Brill), 729–739.

Kugel, J. L. (1981), *The Idea of Biblical Poetry* (New Haven, CT: Yale University Press).

——(1998), *Traditions of the Bible: A Guide to the Bible as It Was at the Start of the Common Era* (Cambridge, MA: Harvard University Press).

——(2007), *How to Read the Bible: A Guide to Scripture Then and Now* (New York: Free Press).

Lau, W. (1994), *Schriftgelehrte Prophetie in Jes 56-66*, BZAW 225 (Berlin: Walter de Gruyter).

Liebreich, L. J. (1956), "The Compilation of the Book of Isaiah," *JQR ns* 46, 259–277.

Lyons, M. (2009), *From Law to Prophecy: Ezekiel's Use of the Holiness Code*, LHBOTS 507 (New York: T&T Clark International).

Machinist, P. (1983), "Assyria and Its Image in First Isaiah," *JAOS* 103, 719–737.

Mathews, C. R. (1995), *Defending Zion: Edom's Desolation and Jacob's Restoration (Isaiah 34-35) in Context*, BZAW 236 (Berlin: Walter de Gruyter).

McKane, W. (1967), "The Interpretation of Isaiah VII 14-15," *VT* 17, 208–209.

Melugin, R. F. (1976), *The Formation of Isaiah 40-55*, BZAW 141 (Berlin: Walter de Gruyter).

Mettinger, T. N. D. (1983), *A Farewell to the Servant Songs. A Critical Examination of an Exegetical Axiom* (Lund: CWK Gleerup).

Middlemas, J. (2005), "Divine Reversal and the Role of the Temple in Trito-Isaiah," in J. Day (ed.), *Temple and Worship in Ancient Israel*, JSOTSup 422 (London: T&T Clark International), 164–187.

Miscall, P. D. (1992), "Isaiah: New Heavens, New Earth, New Book," in D. N. Fewell (ed.), *Reading between Texts: Intertextuality and the Hebrew Bible* [Literary Currents in Biblical Interpretation] (Louisville, KY: Westminster John Knox), 41–56.

Moberly, R. W. L. (2009), "What is Theological Interpretation of Scripture?" *JTI* 3, 161–178.

Moughtin-Mumby, S. (2008), *Sexual and Marital Metaphors in Hosea, Jeremiah, Isaiah, and Ezekiel*, OTM (Oxford: Oxford University Press).

Muilenburg, J. (1956), "The Book of Isaiah: Chapters 40-66," in G. A. Buttrick, W. R. Bowie, P. Scherer, J. Knox, S. Terrien, and N. B. Harmon (eds.), *The Interpreter's Bible 5* (New York: Abingdon Press), 381–776.

Nielsen, K. (1989), *There is Hope for a Tree: The Tree as Metaphor in Isaiah*, JSOTSup 65 (Sheffield: Sheffield Academic Press).

North, C. R. (1950), "The 'Former Things' and the 'New Things' in Deutero-Isaiah," in H. H. Rowley (ed.), *Studies in Old Testament Prophecy Presented to Professor Theodore H. Robinson* (New York: Scribner's), 111–126.

——(1964), *The Second Isaiah* (Oxford: Clarendon Press).

Nurmela, R. (2006), *The Mouth of the Lord Has Spoken: Inner-Biblical Allusions in Second and Third Isaiah*, Studies in Judaism (Lanham,MD: University Press of America).

Plantinga, A. (2000), *Warranted Christian Belief* (New York: Oxford University Press).
Polaski, D. C. (2001), *Authorizing an End: The Isaiah Apocalypse and Intertextuality*, BibIntS 50 (Leiden: Brill).
Rendtorff, R. (1993), "Isaiah 56:1 as a Key to the Formation of the Book of Isaiah," *Canon and Theology* (Minneapolis: Fortress), 181–189.
——(2005), *The Canonical Hebrew Bible: A Theology of the Old Testament*, trans. D. E. Orton (Leiden: Deo Publishing).
Roberts, J. J. M. (1983), "Isaiah 33: An Isaianic Elaboration of the Zion Tradition," in C. L. Meyers and M. O'Connor (eds.), *The Word of the Lord Shall Go Forth: Essays in Honor of David Noel Freedman in Celebration of his Sixtieth Birthday* (Winona Lake, IN: Eisenbrauns), 15–25.
Rosenberg, J. (1975), "Meanings, Morals, and Mysteries: Literary Approaches to the Torah," *Response* 9, 67–94.
Sailhamer, J. (1995), *Introduction to Old Testament Theology: A Canonical Approach* (Grand Rapids, MI: Zondervan).
Schöckel, L. A. (1987), "Isaiah," in R. Alter and F. Kermode (eds.), *The Literary Guide to the Bible* (Cambridge, MA: Harvard University Press), 165–183.
Schultz, R. L. (1999), *The Search for Quotation: Verbal Parallels in the Prophets*, JSOTSup 180 (Sheffield: Sheffield Academic Press).
Seeligmann, I. L. (1953), "Voraussetzungen der Midraschexegese," VTSup 1, 150–181.
Seitz, C. (1988), "Isaiah 1-66: Making Sense of the Whole," in C. Seitz (ed.), *Reading and Preaching the Book of Isaiah* (Philadelphia: Fortress), 105–126.
——(1990), "The Divine Council: Temporal Transition and New Prophecy in the Book of Isaiah," *JBL* 109, 229–247.
——(1991), *Zion's Final Destiny: The Development of the Book of Isaiah* (Minneapolis: Fortress Press).
——(1993), *Isaiah 1-39* (Louisville, KY: John Knox Press).
——(1998), *Word Without End: The Old Testament as Abiding Theological Witness* (Grand Rapids, MI: Eerdmans).
——(2001a), "The Book of Isaiah 40-66," in L. E. Keck (ed.), *NIB* 6 (Nashville, TN: Abingdon), 309–552.
——(2001b), *Figured Out: Typology and Providence in Christian Scripture* (Louisville, KY: Westminster John Knox).
——(2007), *Prophecy and Hermeneutics* (Grand Rapids, MI: Baker Academic).
Skehan, P. W. (1957), "The Qumran Manuscripts and Textual Criticism," *Volume du congres: Strasbourg, 1956*, VTSup 4 (Leiden: Brill), 148–160.
Smith, M. S. (2001), *The Origins of Biblical Monotheism: Israel's Polytheistic Background and the Ugaritic Texts* (New York: Oxford University Press).
Smith, P. A. (1995), *Rhetoric and Redaction in Trito-Isaiah*, VTSup 62 (Leiden: Brill).
Sommer, B. (1998), *A Prophet Reads Scripture: Allusion in Isaiah 40-66* (Stanford, CA: Stanford University Press).
Steck, O. H. (1991), "Tritojesaja im Jesajabuch," *Studien zu Tritojesaja*, BZAW 203 (Berlin: de Gruyter), 3–45.
——(1991b), *Studien zu Tritojesaja*, BZAW 203 (Berlin: Walter de Gruyter).
Stendahl, K. (1962), "Biblical Theology, Contemporary," *The Interpreter's Dictionary of the Bible* 1 (Nashville, TN: Abingdon Press), 418–432.
Sternberg, M. (1985), *The Poetics of Biblical Narrative. Ideological Literature and the Drama of Reading* (Bloomington, IN: Indiana University Press).
Stromberg, J. (2008), "The 'Root of Jesse' in Isaiah 11:10: Postexilic Judah, or Postexilic King?" *JBL* 127, 655–669.

——(2009a), "The Role of Redaction Criticism in the Evaluation of a Textual Variant: Another Look at 1QIsaᵃ XXXII 14 (38:21-22)," *DSD* 16, 155–189.

——(2009b), "The Second Temple and the Isaianic Afterlife of the חסדי דוד (Isa 55, 3-5)," *ZAW* 121, 242–255.

——(2010), *Isaiah after Exile: The Author of Third Isaiah as Reader and Redactor of the Book*, OTM (Oxford: Oxford University Press).

Sweeney, M. A. (1996), *Isaiah 1-39*, FOTL 16 (Grand Rapids, MI: Eerdmans).

——(1997), "Prophetic Exegesis in Isaiah 65-66," in C. Broyles and C. Evans (eds.), *Writing and Reading the Scroll of Isaiah: Studies of an Interpretive Tradition*, VTSup 70,1 (Leiden: Brill), 455–474.

——(2001), *King Josiah: The Lost Messiah of Israel* (New York: Oxford University Press).

——(2010), "Isaiah," in M. D. Coogan (ed.), *The New Oxford Annotated Bible: New Revised Standard Version with the Apocrypha* (New York: Oxford University Press), 965–967.

Teeter, D. A. (2009), "'You Shall Not Seethe a Kid in its Mother's Milk': The Text and the Law in Light of Early Witnesses," *Textus* 24, 36–63.

Tiemeyer, L.-S. (2006), *Priestly Rites and Prophetic Rage: Post-Exilic Prophetic Critique of the Priesthood*, FAT 2nd Series 19 (Tübingen: Mohr Siebeck).

Uhlig, T. (2009), *The Theme of Hardening in the Book of Isaiah*, FAT 2. Reihe 39 (Tübingen: Mohr Siebeck).

Ulrich, E. (2001), "The Developmental Composition of the Book of Isaiah: Light from 1QIsaᵃ on Additions in the MT," *DSD* 8, 288–305.

van Keulen, P. (2010), "On the Identity of the Anonymous Ruler in Isaiah 14:4b-21," in M. N. van der Meer, P. van Keulen, W. van Peursen, and B. t. Haar Romeny (eds.), *Isaiah in Context. Studies in Honour of Arie van der Kooij on the Occasion of his Sixty-Fifth Birthday*, VTSup 138 (Leiden: Brill), 109–123.

Vanhoozer, K. (1998), *Is There a Meaning in this Text? The Bible, the Reader, and the Morality of Literary Knowledge* (Grand Rapids, MI: Zondervan).

von Rad, G. (1965), *Old Testament Theology*, trans. D. M. G. Stalker (New York: Harper & Row).

Watson, W. G. E. (1994), *Traditional Techniques in Classical Hebrew Verse* (Sheffield: Sheffield Academic Press).

Webb, B. G. (1990), "Zion in Transformation: A Literary Approach to Isaiah," in D. J. A. Clines, S. E. Fowl, and S. E. Porter (eds.), *The Bible in Three Dimensions: Essays in Celebration of Forty Years of Biblical Studies in the University of Sheffield*, JSOTSup 87 (Sheffield: Sheffield Academic Press), 65–84.

Wegner, P. (1992), *An Examination of Kingship and Messianic Expectation in Isaiah 1-35* (Lewiston, NY: Mellen).

——(2009), "What's new in Isaiah 9:1-7?" in H. G. M. Williamson and D. G. Firth (eds.), *Interpreting Isaiah: Issues and Approaches* (Nottingham: Apollos), 237–249.

Westermann, C. (1969), *Isaiah 40-66*, trans. D. M. G. Stalker, OTL (London: SCM Press).

Whybray, R. N. (1983), *The Second Isaiah*, OTG (Sheffield: JSOT Press).

Wilcox, P. and D. Paton-Williams. (1988), "The Servant Songs in Deutero-Isaiah," *JSOT* 79–102.

Wildberger, H. (2002), *Isaiah 28-39*, trans. T. H. Trapp (Minneapolis: Fortress).

Williamson, H. G. M. (1978), "'The Sure Mercies of David': Subjective or Objective Genitive?" *JSS* 23, 31–49.

——(1990), "Isaiah 63,7-64,11: Exilic Lament or Postexilic Protest?" *ZAW* 102, 48–58.

——(1993), "First and Last in Isaiah," in H. A. McKay and D. J. A. Clines (eds.), *Of Prophets' Visions and the Wisdom of Sages: Essays in Honour of R. Norman Whybray on his Seventieth Birthday*, JSOTSup 162 (Sheffield: Sheffield Academic Press), 95–108.

——(1994), *The Book Called Isaiah: Deutero-Isaiah's Role in Composition and Redaction* (Oxford: Clarendon).

——(1995), "Synchronic and Diachronic in Isaian Perspective," in J. C. de Moor (ed.), *Synchronic or Diachronic?: A Debate on Method in Old Testament Exegesis* (Leiden: Brill), 211–226.

——(1996), "Hezekiah and the Temple," in M. V. Fox (ed.), *Texts, Temples, and Traditions: A Tribute to Menahem Haran* (Winona Lake, IN: Eisenbrauns), 47–52.

——(1997), "Isaiah 6,13 and 1,29-31," in J. van Ruiten and M. Vervenne (eds.), *Studies in the Book of Isaiah: Festschrift Willem A.M. Beuken* (Leuven: Leuven University Press), 119–128.

——(1998), *Variations on a Theme: King, Messiah and Servant in the Book of Isaiah* (Carlisle: Paternoster Press).

——(2004), "In Search of the Pre-exilic Isaiah," in J. Day (ed.), *In Search of Pre-Exilic Israel: Proceedings of the Oxford Old Testament Seminar*, JSOTSup 406 (London: T&T Clark International), 181–206.

——(2006), *A Critical and Exegetical Commentary on Isaiah 1-27, 1: Isaiah 1-5*, ICC (London: T&T Clark International).

——(2009), "Recent Issues in the Study of Isaiah," in H. G. M. Williamson and D. G. Firth (eds.), *Interpreting Isaiah. Issues and Approaches* (Nottingham: Apollos), 21–39.

Index of Scriptural References

Index of Authors